Edward Fella: Letters on America

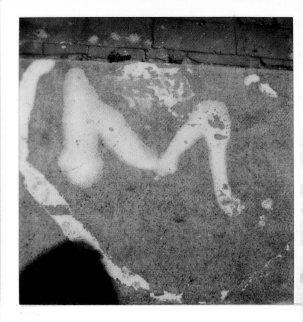

Edward Fella: **Letters on America**

essays by Lewis Blackwell and Lorraine Wild

photographs edited by Lucy Bates

Princeton Architectural Press   New York

Published by   Princeton Architectural Press

37 East Seventh Street
New York, NY 10003
For a catalog of books published by Princeton Architectural Press

call toll-free 800.722.6657   or visit www.papress.com.

Simultaneously
published in London by Laurence King Publishing,
an imprint of Calmann & King Ltd.

Text copyright © 2000 Lewis Blackwell
Text and design © 2000 Lorraine Wild
Images/artwork ©2000 Edward Fella

04 03 02 01 00 5 4 3 2 1 First Edition

Library of Congress Cataloging-in-Publication
Data for this title
is available from the Publisher

ISBN 1-56898-217-8

Printed in Hong Kong

SUNDAY

8 AM 9 AM 11 AM

MONDAY TO FRIDAY

8 AM 12:10 PM 5:30 PM

SATURDAY

10 AM

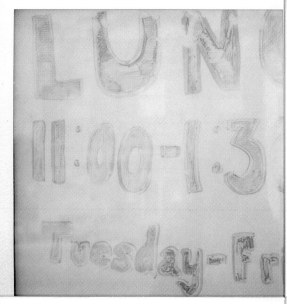

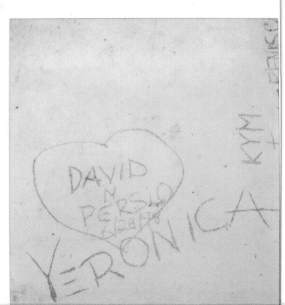

DAVID N PERSID

YERONICA

KYM

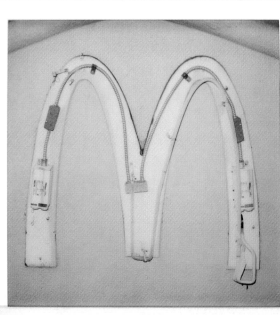

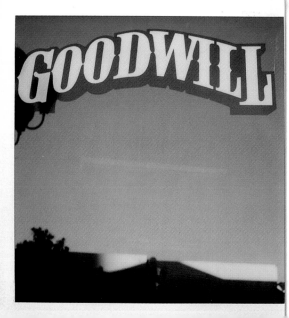

GOODWILL

DUCK CROSSING

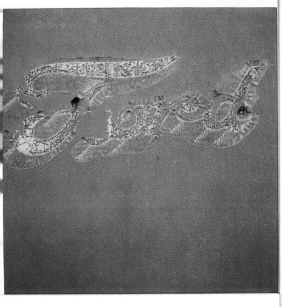

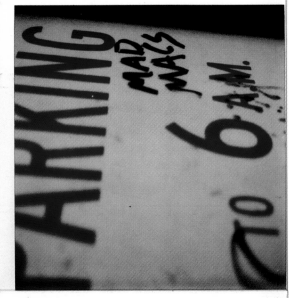
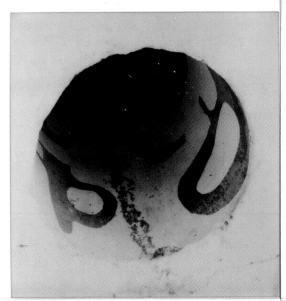

Off The Road by Lewis Blackwell

This book has some pages of hand-drawn lettering in pen and coloured pencil and many pages that show signs in whole or part captured on 1134 photographs shot with a Polaroid 680 SE camera on type 600 film. These drawings and photographs are by Edward Fella (1938–), American born in Detroit; he grew up in the city and worked there as an illustrator and designer until going to graduate school at the age of 47. Shortly after graduation in 1987 he joined the faculty at the California Institute of Arts in Valencia, California. He has lived there ever since, except for time spent on long drives across the United States. Each summer he drives back to the midwest and then on to the east coast. He draws every day in his notebooks, and occasionally designs self-published pieces, but no longer works for clients: at 62, he sees himself at the 'Exit Level' of design, and has no desire or need to work to somebody else's brief.

We walk from the car to the entrance of The Original Saugus Café in Santa Clarita Valley, California: Ed Fella, Lucy Bates and myself. Ed stops suddenly a few paces before the door. He looks with fascination at the adjacent general store, which sports a window full of signs. He says: 'You see, they're everywhere, it's a very American kind of clutter.'

And they are everywhere. In this window, at this moment, a cacophony of characters put on a non-stop visual entertainment proclaiming special offers and surprising services. Beyond this moment they continue coast-to-coast, a vital part of the American experience. These characters, this cast, establish the space and time of big city, small town or roadside passage, as essential in placing us in the 'land of the free' as the highways that stitch together the nation. They are the original 24/7 communication, interactive in ways that the web can't even dream of. The characters can be found on any surface, as distractions or directions, decoration or marker. They are in wood, metal, paint, sticky-back plastic, etched, behind glass, behind bars, torn and layered. They come alone or clustered together, isolated or juxtaposed, fresh or faded, direct or distorted; from in-your-face dayglo to subtle tones that are obscured, reflected, as shadow,

as drop shadow with shadow, or even as a sunburnt memory of a lost message.

These are the letters on America. They are not from it, about it, or out of it…they are literally on it. The product of many hands, of many moments, of many processes. In other countries, there are also splashes of letterforms scattered across the environment, but they are not 'American'. Language, form and place conspire to make them different. Every country has its patina of language repeatedly splattered over its landscape, and every country might justifiably claim a unique quality to its collage of character sets, but they don't approach the same intrusion-level of the sign that is apparent in the United States. Here the very architectural fabric can end up built of signs, in a way only echoed in uncontrolled Third World situations. Here we are atop the imperial power of the First World, the original and best display of twentieth-century, multi-cultural, unfettered free-market capitalist expressionism.

At least since the 1960s, when Robert Venturi and his students mapped the architecture of Las Vegas and suggested modernism could learn something from its facades and furnishings, the vernacular of the graphic environment has become a thing of intellectual study and ironic posturing. But you would be misled to think this book is about the larger message of these signs, about the compositional wholes, or the amusing juxtapositions and contexts of such material. No such populism here. Fella's images are not taken for their amusing language, or their locale. These pictures do not stand back, but come in close. These pictures take us to the smaller messages, the bits in-between, the cracks rather than the compositions. There is no tongue-in-cheek wit or heavy irony here; these are out-takes from work-in-process. They are honestly appreciative, highly respectful of the handiwork, admiring the skill and the accident that went into the marks. This is an important difference to the love of the vernacular that has seeped through recent graphic design: there is no sneer or condescension to the material here, but rather a fascination with its inner workings.

While looking up close, with personal interest in subsuming these details into his own work, Fella is highly conscious that the parts betray more and thereby spin out the greater import of this barrage of unique detail. These images show a ubiquitous but often ignored aspect of America as it is, up close, as we stroll past it, voyeurs of the sidewalk. The images give us many clues to puzzles that lie beyond the picture frame. Fella, so experienced in the commercial forms of illustration and design, self-conscious of just how sophisticated and yet also how limited his own hand skills are, gathers these snaps as prizes from a treasure trove to be reinvested in later work. To put them here is almost a betrayal of their purpose…except that their forms can still live again and again, consciously or subconsciously, in the everyday sketches he works out, every day. The lettering pages interspersing the image blocks illuminate that transition, revealing how the raw becomes the cooked in 'Fellaland'.

America, unlike Europe, for the most part does not have urban space that is made up from the accretion of building forms over many centuries. Instead, the rich layering of most of the built environment has arrived with the industrial and post-industrial age, and in doing so it has come within the time of mass-print and mass-communication. Thus signage is a part of the environment, of the built form, a part of the tradition in a way that does not apply in the capitals or small towns of old Europe. Even in new towns in Europe, historical reference is not to richly signed environments but to the accreted stone, brick and cement of traditional forms, and so the copies aspire to an unsigned territory. In contrast, the new American mall incorporates layers of sign and facade, images and texts, as part of the vernacular it seeks to reference. Europe aspires to a land of Transylvanian mystery, while the United States is a sporting event with the sponsors and scorekeeping to the fore. Neither is more or less fake, but both are perhaps slightly more self-conscious than their precedents.

The café that Fella, Lucy Bates and I finally stepped into was one of the oldest places around Valencia and it dates as far back, perhaps, as the 1930s. The signs help you connect with it, being the visual cry of the seller and at the same time the assertion of the owner, and these help to delimit the space. Meanwhile, in the new mall down the road a tableaux of valley life from the time of the founding of the café is played out in

rich colours across giant murals that are just a couple of years old: again, the sign is saying 'community' while it is also attending to its need to sell, and to assert ownership.

In this culture built on the liberating virtues of trade, it is not surprising that the commercial sign has such a robust, expressive quality, and is so ubiquitous. You can find the same things happening in Europe, Asia and elsewhere, but they are different: signs carry a lot of other baggage besides their overt message. In Europe the sign often speaks of community with a socialist tinge, even in this post-socialist age, and before that it references community with a medieval weight, feudal, oozing associations that you can't question: the values are communal in the grandest and most oppressive political sense. Somehow in America it would not be surprising if a road sign was sponsored, private and yet approachable, whereas in western Europe that would be an affront to the sense of communal values, the desire for authority but not ownership.

Most of the subject matter here is insistently one-off, not private but not in public ownership either; it is more often than not selling goods or services. Usually the signs are for small enterprises, and seem only a few steps from the salesman importuning passers-by. The inflection of the hawker's voice is there in the infinite variety of this lettering. The hoarse comment, the smooth tones, the cries in competition in the marketplace…the ceaseless individualism of vocal expression is matched but with an even greater level of perceptible detail; Fella's camera hones in not so much on the word, as on the individual letterforms and the spaces between, before and behind them.

These 1,100 or so images are less than a third of the collection amassed by Fella since he first started this series of Polaroids in 1987. The project of capturing vernacular lettering detail in this way began on a study trip to San Francisco in the spring of that year, as he approached the end of his master's degree at Cranbrook Academy of Art in Michigan. A mid-life career shift, breaking from the thirty years spent as an illustrator and designer in Detroit, had taken Fella back to graduate school to study on one of the leading graphic design courses in the States. The pioneering mapping of post-modern theory over graphics at the school had fuelled Fella's work, pushing his earlier explorations into more extreme paths: his highly disrupted typographic pieces stood out for their quirkiness that went beyond formal disruption and expressed (thanks to the designer's natural felicity with the pen borne from years of commercial practice) a deep appreciation of vernacular forms.

This appreciation came not through overt professional practice or appropriation. 'I was never one of those designers who was doing "vernacular". I was a highly paid commercial illustrator working for the likes of General Motors, not the corner grocery store!' he says. Indeed, it is not the 'vernacular' as a concept that draws Fella. 'It's not that this stuff is the vernacular, it is not its "on the street" aspect or what it literally says that concerns me. It is the formal qualities of the lettering that particularly interest me.' In this he admits his curiosity is with an arcane corner of the bigger picture. 'I love the mythology of America, including the dark side, but this is more a take on Americana rather than America.'

Ed claims that the material for his images is not hard to find. It isn't (in that material like this is everywhere) and yet it is, in that each image is unique, based on signs that are nearly all one-offs. And as Polaroids, they are originals. They are as rare as people and as unique. This variety is achieved through the surfaces: wood, glass, paper, metal, stone, plaster, cement, tiles, tarmac, plastics and brick. Commonplace. However, many different techniques are overlaid on the surfaces: machine-set type, stencil lettering, lettering incised with a tool, pre-formed stuck lettering, hand-made sticky lettering, painted or drawn (in many fluids and with different tools). Then there are the preformed units of neon, or fabricated metal, glass and wood…factory fabrications made unique by their particular placement in a particular environment over a particular time. There are these variables to consider before we get to describing the individual nature of the characters: perhaps a familiar font, or a common stencil, but also an entirely individual product of one artist or artisan's hand, practised or hamfisted.

What has been done here, in a project of some dozen years so far, is not a documentary, but an insight into 'work in progress'. This is not a book of neatly-taken photographs documenting the roadside vernacular, observing with wry detachment the amusing juxtaposition of message. Other people have done that with funnier observations, more sentimentality.

At first glance the potency of these images comes from a combination of sentimentality and transgression. But only at first glance. Sentimentality because they are documents that savour material so often 'seen' but passed over. We find when looking closer at the roadside gallery that there are strange stitches in the fabric of these canvases. These prompt awareness of the individual at work in the passage of the days, call for respect for the unique if modest visions suspended in time and space, however arbitrary or inexplicable. A warm rush of humanity at work pours out of every shaped and misshapen sign. And even when the 'sign' is an accident of nature—for example, the suggestion of letterforms carried in seaweed on a beach, or soap suds drying and separating into glyphs on a window—the human is still there in the recording eye. We are touched by the person who made the sign, and by Ed Fella making the picture. The images require us to dwell on time past and our collective place in it. We are made aware of the making of space, and we may appreciate that it is a little ironic that two-dimensional imagery (for the most part) enables this.

Transgression? Because for the greater part these images are of things that are not meant to be seen for what they are, but for what they say. When we look at these signs like this, we are looking for too long and too intrusively. They are humdrum and unassuming pointers to other experience, not the stuff of focus. As with most signs, they are meant to be transparent in their messaging, to be consumed as useful or occasionally pleasurable. They are not meant to demand more than a millisecond of thought about their existence, but instead to take our thoughts elsewhere, answering needs or prompting desires.

In itself the self-conscious signing of signs is not transgressive now: for more than thirty years it has been a staple of western cultural speculation; it is mixed into the rubble of thought that underpins post-modernism. The transgression comes in what Fella has done to the signs. He is not really interested in what the signs say, nor is he trying to say that looking at signs closely is in itself remarkable; he is showing these images not as an environmental documentary, but as documents of his thought processes, his looking for the glue that holds these messages together. He is noting the bizarre tics of the temporal, he is seeking out the order in the disorder, the moment that put one letter that way instead of another. Across the Polaroids in these pages a million and more modest yet disruptive questions can be asked—why is that orange painted next to that dull orange plastic, itself next to that blue swashy P on bleached wood? For what reason the struggle to echo machine forms in hand practice to make a sign for sacks? Why is it more than OK to have a big O like that O? How is an A there? Countless variations in letterform and context are contained within these pages. And the result is not images that build to a finished work, but works behind work-in-progress. They are part of the artist's process flayed and displayed. They feed new lettering and image-making. The pages of Fella's penmanship included in this book (examples of his ceaseless outpouring of lettering and images) give the final resting places of some of the ideas. The glitches in the signs are remade, remixed and bedded down into new forms, unique and yet highly referential.

The transgressive act is to pinpoint previously unappreciated (and thereby valueless) difference and raise it to the level of significance. As a result we celebrate—even fetishize—the kinks of message-making, the bits that are not on the programme, but are as vital as the approved system. It may not seem such a big thing as transgressions go, but these pictures are constantly giving value to that which is commonly seen as having no value, or is even seen as being of negative worth.

This is a tendency familiar in graphic design, and indeed in Fella's own career. From appreciating unfashionable illustration and lettering styles at the beginning of his commercial art career in the late 1950s, to exploring the concern about irregular spacing prompted by early computer typography in the late 1980s when he began teaching at CalArts (Fella doesn't use a computer to this day), there is a constant quest to embrace that which rubs things the wrong way. It is a familiar form of transgressive behaviour: that which is prohibited, or repressed, is first revealed or rediscovered as covertly attractive, then openly if controversially embraced, then celebrated as part of a new value system. It is the fact that we don't normally see these elements in the signs—that we repress them from being of importance in our reading of the signs—that makes them significant. Our enjoyment (if that is the right word) in dwelling on these images is that we thrill to see that which is not normally seen. It is all the better for being previously unaccounted.

That is at first glance. But when the thrill has gone, when the warm glow of sentiment at seeing this familiar stuff made a little unfamiliar dies down, what do we have at second glance? We see that the choice of image subject is not arbitrary, nor is it tied to a programme. It is structured around the idea that these are things Fella can use. These are ideas.

He comes in close with his camera, a camera deliberately chosen for its restricted but unique functionality, capable of almost instantly delivering a regularly formatted image with a good fixed lens, the image flashlit or not, focused here or there but always subject to the colour palette and resolution of type 600 film. The compositions are precisely controlled, and yet the final images are not always so precisely worked. Fella typically only takes one shot of a subject, and has discarded very few images over the,dozen years of the series. If an image ends up a little blown out by the flash, so be it, that's part of that moment for that sign.

Given what he is recording, it is not surprising that precision and imprecision are held in tension in the making of the pictures. Fella is carefully looking at the bits that we would normally subconsciously erase—the irregular spacing, the unplanned juxtaposition of surface, the weathered image that sits next to an incongruous character. He finds and cherishes the events that make each sign unique, appreciating them not for what they say, or for their historical significance, or for any programmed reason, but instead appreciating them for the thing he can use. That is all there is: ideas you might want to re-shape, recycle, reformat, or even occasionally revolt against.

While Fella has an archive of photographs in this book, he did not take them in order to build an archive, but to be notes towards later image-making. Even when this book was in development, and he knew that certain photographs might work to build out certain themes, he could not work out how to 'assign' himself to these tasks. The subject choice for photography is not derived from a programme, but is impulsion drawn from that rich experience and aspiration as to the value of these signs. 'In part, these photographs are about nothing more than what letters look like when they are photographed,' says Fella. And that is a statement that can be taken to mean nothing more than it says on the surface, or can be examined, like the image, for its own grain.

There is virtually no difference between what the original subject is and what Fella ends up with as his image. Having seen something that seems remarkable, he takes it, with care and increasing skill over the years. He throws away virtually nothing after the decision to photograph has been made. This is unlike any conventional professional practice. 'I haven't thrown away more than a handful of pictures in all the years. Hey, they cost a dollar each!', jokes Fella, but it is a true laugh: the money was never immaterial, and neither was the appreciation that the photograph is itself the object.

Of course, to get the collection down to a size that could squeeze into this book took editing, but there were as many on the table fighting to be in as ended up here. The images at the basic level of image-making document signs that are of equal value: they are what they are. They are one Polaroid's worth of sign. The challenge for the editors of this book was to arrive at some more sophisticated (but certainly not absolute) values.

'The pictures are deliberately, precisely, composed,' Fella says. 'I am not particularly interested in the words, indeed I deliberately cut off parts of the words or letters. It is very spontaneous, but also very composed. Each photo has its own investment for me, each was made for a reason: it is difficult for me to say that one is good or that one is bad.'

'I use low design to make high design, non-condescendingly,' he stresses. 'It's a kind of bio-feedback; it's visual reference material at its simplest.' The appropriation involved in this image-making is an appreciation, albeit a critique too. And then a further appropriation, and heightening, may take place if that subsequently feeds through into the design and art work. This is a deep, transformational appreciation for object (the sign) and subject (Fella as artist).

He admits to sometimes 'theorizing after the fact', realizing the powers of what he has photographed or what has fed through into his work after the event of shooting that image or making a letterform. 'I have this idea that I'm taking these pictures because I'm going to do some kind of future project around it.' Which, in several ways, he has…and continues to do each time he opens up a sketchbook and creates letterforms and related elements that draw on the accumulated appreciation of the vernacular forms and practices.

The images in themselves, though, and in their shaping and making, can be analysed for an intricacy of vision and craft which reveals much about the Polaroid project as a whole. While ostensibly all concerned with the same subject, they contain within them great differences that go beyond the raw content (the sign) being shown. For one thing, the signs are sometimes shouting out their oddity, but in other cases it is Fella who has brought the 'idea' to the sign. This was definitely the case with the first images in his project, which were street signs in San Francisco that were photographed in such a way as to particularly emphasize the stretch and squash possibilities of foreshortening in photography. The signs in themselves were less remarkable (standard US road signs in several cases) but recording what the eye sees (or what the eye sees as the camera can capture) brought out a range of 'typographic' effects that pre-date the digital experiments that designers would undertake *en masse* with desktop graphics software over the following few years.

Those images are, however, atypical. The bulk of the series preoccupies itself with more one-off signs and collisions. Here, the images fall into at least two areas. There are those which report, and there are those which reveal. In this the images sit squarely in the territory of documentary photography.

On the one hand, the selection is made to capture something of note, to report it as it ties in with issues that Fella thinks are interesting (such as irregular spacing, the curious freedoms of hand lettering, a strange distressed effect, some obscuring of characters, the fall of shadow). They are not documents taken with a view for others to see: they are not commissioned, or devised to inform anybody other than Fella's own sensibility.

Then there is the more artful image that demonstrably seeks to reveal a point to us. These use the power of the crop or the fall of light to make a point: for example, images of non-text marks that can be interpreted as having characteristics akin to letters; or damaged signs whose unplanned marks have started to take on pictorial qualities (such as the rusting face seemingly eating one sign, or the melodramatic film-like, movie title, effect of shooting incised letters at an angle with shadow falling across them). Those that reveal, that shape and make a point, go beyond the report level of meaning that perhaps describes most of the pictures.

In stressing this more 'intentional' element in the picture meaning, I tread on thin ground. After all, as suggested above, Fella takes these pictures fairly quickly, on the fly as he walks along. Once taken, the camera is placed in his bag or pocket and Fella walks on. So to suggest that he is determined to reveal certain elements, shaping the picture to carry a particular personal message could seem to be misrepresenting the process. However, the decisive act of taking a picture determines that there is a very specific meaning, however difficult to retrieve. This rediscovery is not easy in that Fella is quite consciously 'not really interested in the meaning of the words, or the wit of word juxtapositions. Other people have done that, and it is certainly not something I ever wanted to do with these pictures. In fact of the very few I have thrown away it is sometimes because of what it inadvertently said.'

So what are the pictures about? Can we find some unifying theme? Are these pictures about art, or about design? In that they have no compulsion to respect the integrity of the original (in other words, the signs are nearly always carefully cropped to disrupt the original message) they can scarcely be reporting on the art or design that may be within the source subject. In that they are not a completed work or with any clear sense of defined purpose, the images would not seem to fit art or design.

At this point, the images and sketches might seem to be of such uncontrolled meaning as to have no clear message…and to be of little or no value other than eye candy for people who like spotting the curious detail of signs. However, this leads us to the label that most readily might be given: that these images and drawings record and then rework the vernacular. But think beyond the twee box that the word 'vernacular' has come to sit in. This is not about noting and appropriating. While Fella knows how to do that, there is an altogether more discursive programme at work. The images are mapping out a territory of new meanings (but visual meanings to which you cannot put easy words) and every image and sketch is a possible position for the evolution of language. Fella's documents are scout's maps showing the edge of visual language, where it builds up and breaks down, where it can go. They are the sighting of stars at the edge of the known universe; suddenly we see how A and Q can sit together and suggest something unexpected. From such little bricks and mortar large edifices of meaning can grow.

Remembering Fella's comment 'it's a take on Americana that I am doing, rather than America,' we can see it is an occasional meditation on the language that shapes our sense of America. This Americana, these telling quirks of everyday clutter that speak of and define a whole nation and its culture, these are outpourings and aspirations washed on the littered shore of the roadside; it is the opposite of high culture, it is the mythical, dream dimension of American visual culture that emerges from the ephemeral.

And let's not overlook Fella's use of the word 'take'. This is a variation, and there could have been others. This is not a finite statement. The meaning of this work can be found by looking at its use. It is not art, it is not design: such work is identified by its use as such. For with these photographs and drawings, which could have been art or design if used differently, the meaning comes from what we (or Fella) do with them. And what we all do with them is take them as something to inform, to feed or fuel the process by which we work with letters. The drawings which may themselves be fed by the pictures, or the pictures which may be fed by the mind that makes the drawings, are material for further mutation from any ideas of an absolute letterform, any sense of 'correct' usage for language. These pages show visual language evolving.

This book, with its thousand variant letterforms, is at the opposite pole from a finished dictionary or any other kind of systemized reference work. It celebrates the 'either/or' nature of things, and is entirely open-ended. It reinforces our understanding of the meanings in specific letterforms or words or sentences by helping us understand the variations. Through seeing the diversity we sense the parameters of the visual language that shapes our vision.

No values are proscribed or prescribed in this process. We take from this what is...and Fella's curious 'take' on it, through the making of these pictures and drawing of characters, says that 'what is' keeps changing, shifting, finding new ways of pushing the signs further.

On almost my final day visiting Ed and Lucy to prepare this book, after a lunch in a new 'Italian' restaurant accessed off the main mall, we stroll through the almost instant town centre that Valencia has acquired: it's a state-of-the-art piece of suburban thinking, featuring a range of options for the shopper-driver. Instead of the straight car park exiting to the stores, here routes and required behaviour give a more sophisticated simulation of how it is in nice old towns. Cars are allowed to mingle a little, enough to dress the main streets without causing a traffic jam or excessive danger. The mix of architecture and routes is just enough to give a sense of place that goes beyond this being simply a developer's plan for farming a collection of shops and restaurants.

One store stands out, physical reference of an earlier conversation, and we go in. Here in a darkened space hushed shoppers pay homage and often money to the genius of Thomas Kinkade, Master of Light™. On the walls, the sentimental, warm-toned, painting-effect prints of the master's work are for sale at four-figure prices and presented with the aura of being originals despite being in editions of many hundreds. Thomas not surprisingly looks pleased with himself on the video, which is also for sale. This store is one of a chain of dealers across the States, peddling Kinkade's visions of a mythical America, landscapes mostly with the occasional nostalgic city scene, nothing too recent, all warmly in the memory, the stuff of an old Hallmark card half-remembered and mixed in with a vacation.

Ed, an occasional collector of naive landscape paintings, delights (very knowingly) in the professional 'naivety' of Kinkade's work. His standpoint, as with his work, is not cynical but somehow admiring and critical. The polished populism of the operation impresses, while the images and their forms are a rich and amusing area to deconstruct. He finds much to enjoy. It would be hard to think of an artist and work at more distance from Fella's own take on the vernacular, and yet at some point the photographs in this book, even the lettering, and Kinkade's kitsch paintings are joined. The painting-prints strive to be, and succeed in being, the taste of popular America. But the imagery in this book is, inadvertently, just as much about the taste of popular America as revealed through every sign along our journey. It maps the tension between the individual and the community, between the impenetrable personal language and the cliché of common language. And in Fella's own lettering, this everyday tension finds a remarkable expression—hovering elusively between the impenetrability of the wholly unique and the transparency of the wholly understood.

These images open us out to an unfinished, unending, experience and invite us to recognize the way the street feeds our eyes in more ways than language has methods of defining. As we look at these records of words and marks, we find that any meaning we give them dissolves into something altogether more primordial, from whence the urge to make marks emerges. For all that we may discuss these pictures, we cannot interpret them in the sense of capturing their meaning: we can only use them as they breed within us. They are used signs, meant to be used. And as we recognize them, we see a little of ourselves. We start to feel the hidden language of America as we assemble the grammar of these signs, a language of commerce that is within and without the individual.

take a spinning rest of a lifetime of art

Contents

17

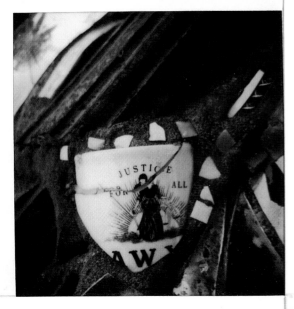

ertin
hers
WELERS

ENTRANCE

OPEN

Caulfield
ART
GALLERY

Bob Slater
Stationer

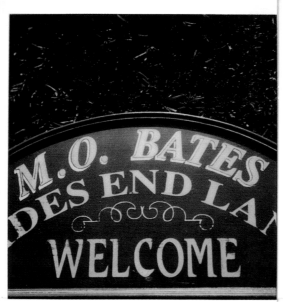

M.O. BATES
DES END LA
WELCOME

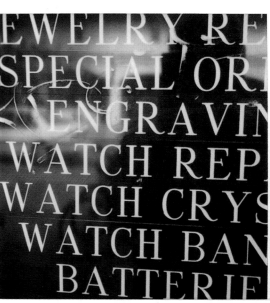

EWELRY RE
SPECIAL OR
ENGRAVIN
WATCH REP
WATCH CRYS
WATCH BAN
BATTERIE

Brian
S
B

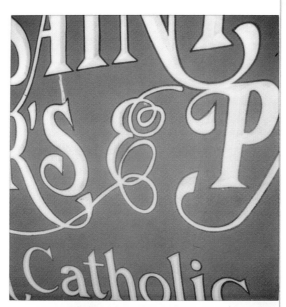

AINT
R'S & P
Catholic

TAURAN

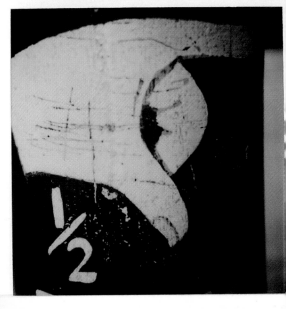

DIEBOLD SAFE & LOCK

CANTON.O.

AMUSEMENTS

ARENAC COUNTY

FAIR

FAIRGROUNDS

JULY

CARDS

VINS

FIGURE

H WAY R

SIQUE

NAIL SALON

Thru Courtyard

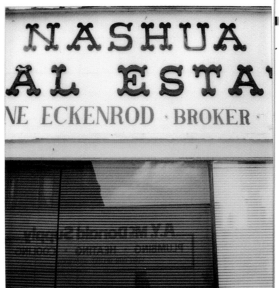

NASHUA

AL ESTA

NE ECKENROD · BROKER

MIRAMA

MARKET

★ DELI

★ SANDWICHES

★ COFFEE

RM MACH

RRIAGES,

WICH SHELLERS   M

AND

Y PRESSES   BIN

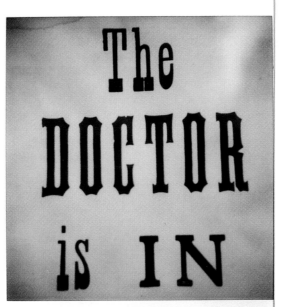

The

DOCTOR

is IN

Nashua Reporter

co-owners:

D

Orric

Conklin

D.O.C. Ltd.

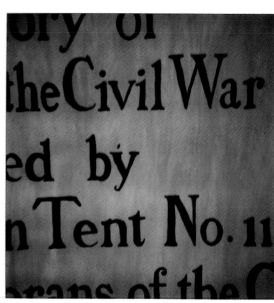

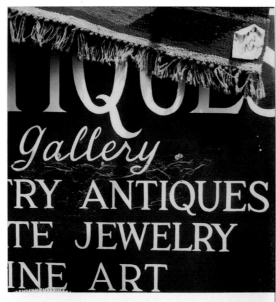

TAPPETS TO BE SET
O THOUSANDTHS
→FRONT←
FIRING ORDER
1-5-3-6-2-4

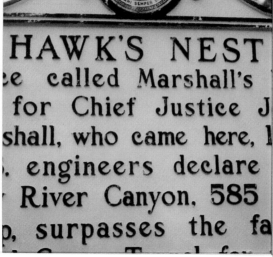

HAWK'S NEST
ee called Marshall's
for Chief Justice J
shall, who came here,
engineers declare
River Canyon. 585
o, surpasses the fa

GEO. B. TRIPLATS
SILVER STATE
ORE CAR
PAT. JAN. 8, 1893
AUG. 27, 1895. JULY
IN CANADA JUNE 2
MFD BY
MFG. CO.
DENVER, COLO.

CITY
OF
CHICAGO

HE LAID THE FOUNDAT
SERVICE. DEFINING AND
UNDER WHICH ITS AREA
CONSERVED UNIMPAIR
THERE WILL NEVER CO

K PARK
LA PITS
ENTED TO
LOS ANGELES, C
MBER 1916 BY

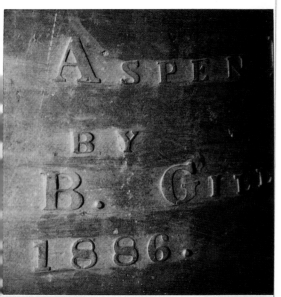

ASPEN
BY
B. GIL
1886.

NTH STREET BR
ERECTED 1925-1926
LLEGHENY COUNT

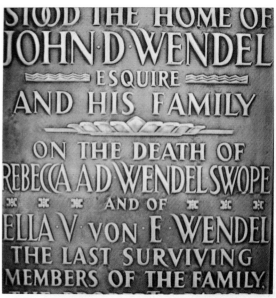

STOOD THE HOME OF
JOHN D WENDEL
ESQUIRE
AND HIS FAMILY
ON THE DEATH OF
REBECCA A D WENDEL SWOPE
AND OF
ELLA V von E WENDEL
THE LAST SURVIVING
MEMBERS OF THE FAMILY.

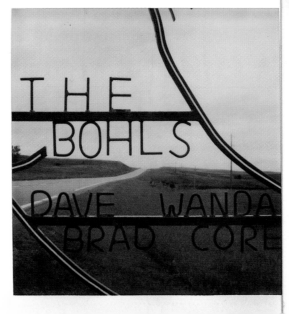

MALARKEY NETWORK NOW TIME FLANGED TO A

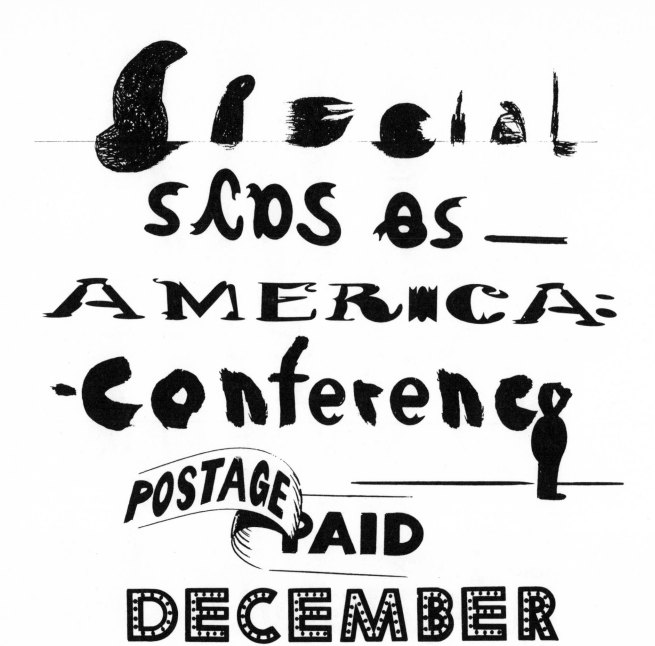

TRAIL
REVEG

ARTISTS
VARIOUS MINERA
VOLCANIC DEPOSI
PINKS AND YELLO
GREEN. MANGANES
ON THE PALETTE

DIXSON
WALKWA

10 W DRUCKER
12W. TODD
14W. M. HELGESON
16 W WILSON

FIRE
TE HIG

keep them b
you of certain
area and is not
nd, athletic field, o
dogs, cars, metal
not permi

HEIGHT ABOVE
RESERVOIR A
RESERVOIR C
CREST LENGT
CREST WIDTH

PLEASANT CYN
WINGATE RD.
GOLER WASH 15
INDIAN RANC
HAPPY
SURPRISE

Riviera
Supper
Club
Open 5 p.m.

STATE
HIGHWAY
BEGINS
HERE

BAY Ri
y
REAL ES
876 - 888

The
DEPOT
SUPPER CLUB

AS B
SH O
ENTRAN

The SEN

THE
LACE
ANOR
30

RYSTA

AKWOO
MANOR
885

THE
PLACE
ESL 929
VENTUCOPA

hiropra
For1P
ry Clea
Hairstyl

argie
Arr

ERNS
RANCE
1991 →

WHALL
PET
CLINIC

IN MEM
SAMUEL
+ CLASS

ORN IN CHICAG
IED IN BOSTO

Mich

RE

  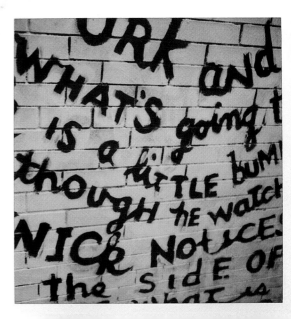

CRANE PLUMBING
AND
SUPPLY

Built
1894

TIVE SEWING
457-4452

CLOSED

Jares
AT THE SHOR

38

MICHIGAN
CHANDELIER
COMPANY

6580

TICKETS AND
INFORMATION
UPSTAIRS
IN GALLERY

BO

FLEA
MARKET

PIÑON

KITCHENS

MOTEL

no Park

PRIVATE
PARKING
UNAUTHORIZED
CARS WILL BE

D TOWN
BARBECUE
May 3-4

COLO.

FAMILY
MEATS

AMISH
FRYERS
1.29 LB.
CLOSED

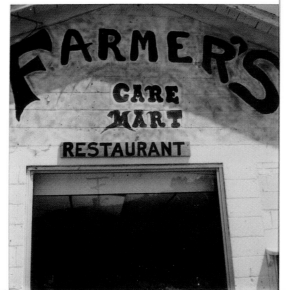
FARMER'S
CARE
MART
RESTAURANT

SOUVENIRS
INDIAN GOODS
JEWELRY
BASKETS
MOCCASINS

CLIMB THE TOWER
VIEW THE
MACKINAC
BRIDGE

JEWEL DINER
DINING ROOM

414 416
HAYWOOD BERK
FLOOR COMPANY

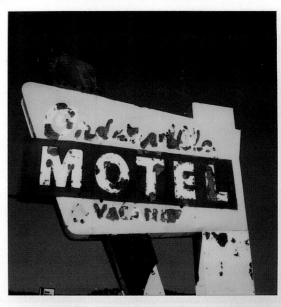

HELP ME!!
I WANT TO BE A
? ? STORE
PHONE: (712) 852-3385

PRIME inc.

The
Flower
Basket

DISHWASHER/
PREP PERSON
WANTED!
_____
_____

Full time

Full Time
Hostess/Busser
WANTED!!
_____

OP

E BEST
34

T LITT
35

STOR
36

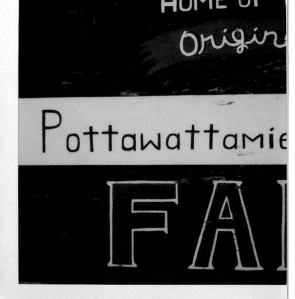

HOME OF
Origin
Pottawattamie
FAAIR

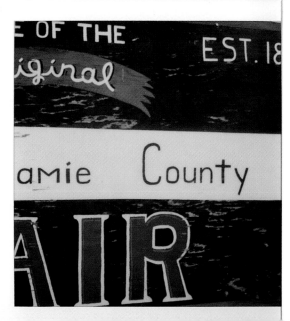

E OF THE
EST. 18
iginal
amie County
AIR

RIGHT HERE
MOTEL AND
RESTAURANT
BEST IN TOWN
ALL QUEEN BEDS

LODGING
COLD·CREEK·I
DINING
LOUNGE
UR DJ KARAOKE
FRI SAT

GROWN
TOMATOE GARLIC
SELF·SERVE
Apricots

FREE
es -FREE - $16 ft. of Selected merchan
Limit-3 Items

GALLERY
OPEN
Q

COME IN
FOR
SOME GIFT
IDEAS
FATHER'S
DAY
JUNE 16th

LARGE GERANIUMS
Flower
Market ←
Rose Bushes

CAR
WASH
DONATIONS
PLEASE
FIRST
ASSEMBLY
YOUTH

TANGE RINES
SWEET, JUICY 4 LB. $1.00
KIWI 4-$1.00
PPLES FIREWOO

DET

RO IT

I&C   AUT
             FO
             D
ENGINE   S
BRAKES   OI

SERV

AMERICAN
CYCLE

AN
MART

COTTON

REPAIR

The Styling
882-55733

TO REPAIR
FOREIGN &
DOMESTIC
SUSPENSION
L CHANGE
ICE 773-549-8254

Warren
Building

L. King

N BELT

RUGS
GEHRIG'S
TAXIDERM
AME
HEADS
2 1/2 BLOCKS

FISH
HRIG'S
DERMY
LIFE
SIZE
S NORTH →

Toys,
ANTIQUE
Collecta
old Records

Rs Sale
looNey ST
ools,
EN WARE

REPAIR

Graphic Designer And

A CALARTS

GRAPHFUS Design PROGRAM EVENT

OUT OF EGO

LODES OF RICHES

PRESENTS
Typographers'
Wedn. Day
Paganini
Natur lick
COLLABORATIONS

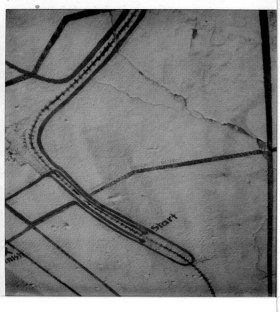

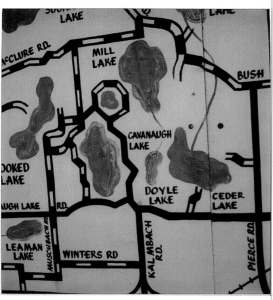

SOUTH LAKE
LAKE
McCLURE RD.
MILL LAKE
BUSH
CROOKED LAKE
CAVANAUGH LAKE
AUGH LAKE
RD.
DOYLE LAKE
CEDER LAKE
LEAMAN LAKE
WINTERS RD
KALMBACH RD.
PIERCE RD.

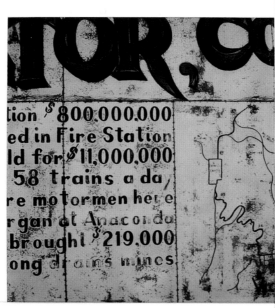

TOR, Co

tion $800,000,000
ed in Fire Station
ld for $11,000,000
58 trains a day
re motormen here
rgan at Anaconda
brought $219,000
ong drains mines

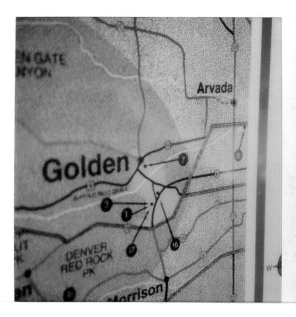

Arvada

Golden

DENVER
RED ROCK
PK

Morrison

OHIO ou BELLE RIVIERE

THE FORT WAS DEST

tah Lake
Prov
h Fork

DONNER PEAK
DONNER PASS
OLD HIGHWAY 40

design excellence

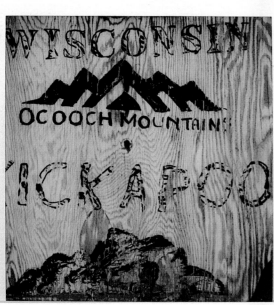

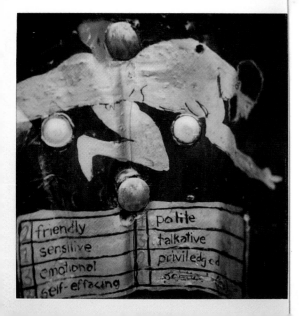

CALARTS

CalArts

CALARTS

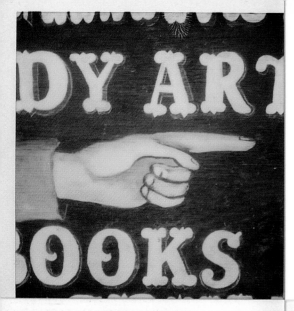

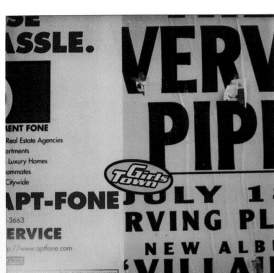

Corned on Rye with Swiss $4.00

Bagels, Bagels, Bagels!

Homemade Cinnamon Rolls Daily

Specialty Wine Shoppe

Cafe Seating!

nie '96

WANDER ARE LOST

WHATEVER CRISPIES ME TO

Cloverleaf

DRINK PEPS GET STUFF

diet PEPSI

pop

pop

Breakfast Served All DAY!!

BOOTHS AVAILABLE IN OUR NEW DINING ROOM

DEGREES

EZCD

JOKER ★ FIVE ★ SPEED

ALONE

SPIRIT GUIDE

Skarhead KINGS AT CRIME NEW YORK CITY THUG CORE

FLEX

communicated

Skarhead KINGS AT CRIME NEW YORK CITY THUG CORE

CONDITIONERS

CA$H

RO

TO-OWN

CHARGED livin' large

HAVE SOUL

Premium

Grain Be

HAWKEYES
Compliments of your Farm Bureau Insurance Agent

TEXAS GOAT ROPER

DINING ROOM

NO SMOKING

"IS THIS HEAVEN?" IOWA

L E

Jewelry

Vintage & New Clothing

OPEN

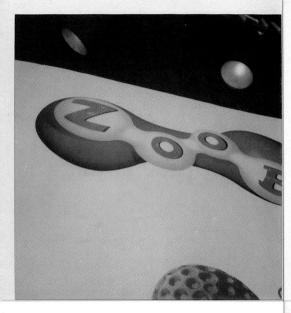

Detroit DETROIT FOCUS GALLERY

FOCUS Gallery

743 BEAUBIEN

3RD FLOOR

DETROIT MICHIGAN 48226

CONTINUUM

DETROIT

FOCUS

Lunches

11:00   2:00

Yes WE'R

OURS

M-4:30PM
ON

...COME

SEE US!

9 to 430pm

naq

A Long Step Back
JIM COSTA
GMS GRAD.

DONALDS
EANIE
EANIES

CLOSED

PAN ALLEY

TAI

Dry
Cleaning

BUS TO
WELCO

OM

OFC. SPC./584

FO

ITCHEN

Homemad
Watermelo

PA
"La
-B

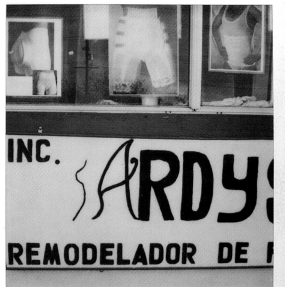

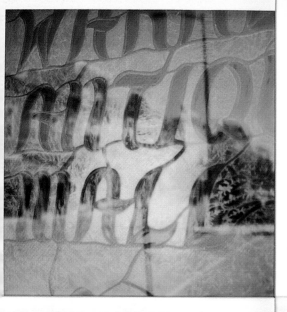

LICENSED LLBO
RI MALAYSIA
ESTAURANT

PUBLIC
REST ROOMS
DOWNSTAIRS

OPEN

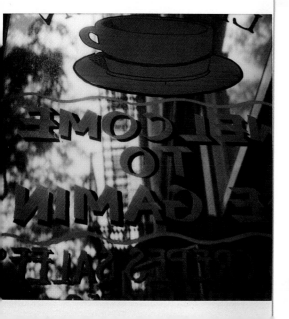

AIR
CONDITIONED
DINING ROOM
In Rear

MARKET

teacher:
"Rules are taught
TO Be broken
only
EXCEPTionally"
Exceptionally"
UnEXPECTANTly"

THIS IS What WILL NEVER DO BECAUSE DO IS WHAT this NEVER WILL.

incredible I look at here

Tuesday, portfolio help them at celebrate. Beursschouwburg

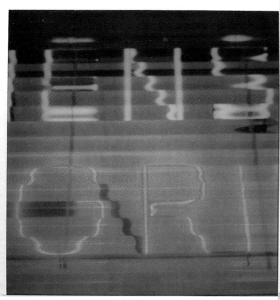

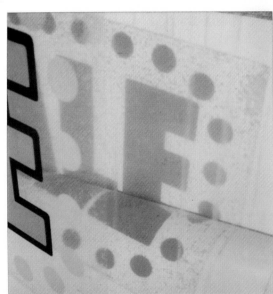

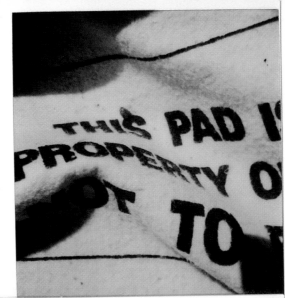

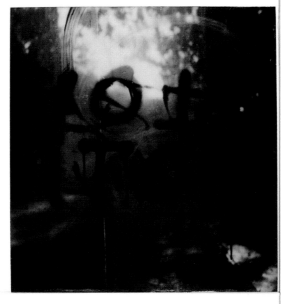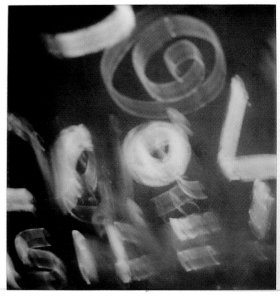

Before the Seeding

All My Letters of Credit

After the Harvest

Take it strong to the hole you have made it & you are B here.

 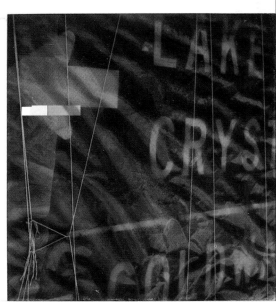 

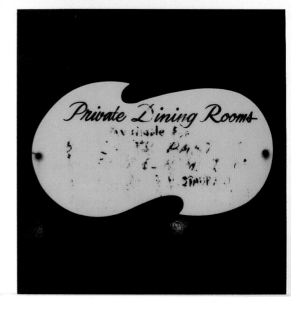

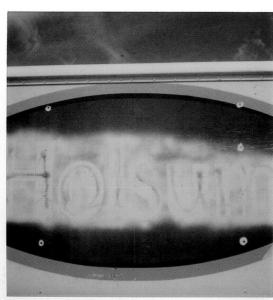

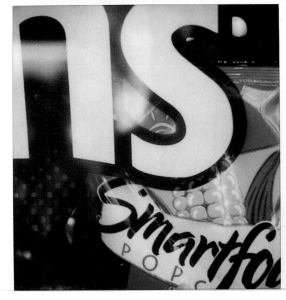

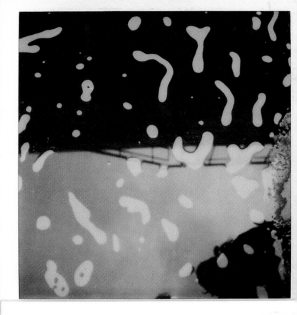

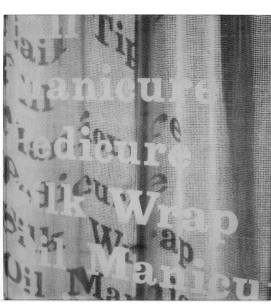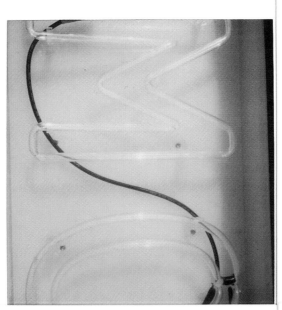

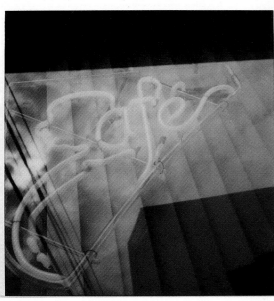

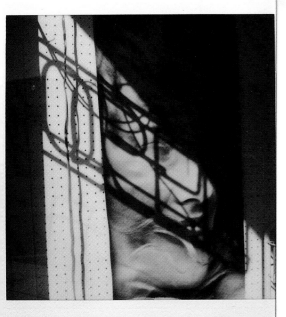

ERMONT GENERAL STORE

OUR BEST

GILLINGHAM & SONS

BURIED

OF

RAULT

PHOT

STUDIO

Greg

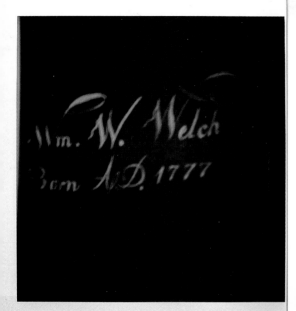

Wm. W. Welch

Born A.D. 1777

Hinkle

1986

OIL
CHANG

CITYPE '99

Stanford

Stanford

Mr.KEEdy

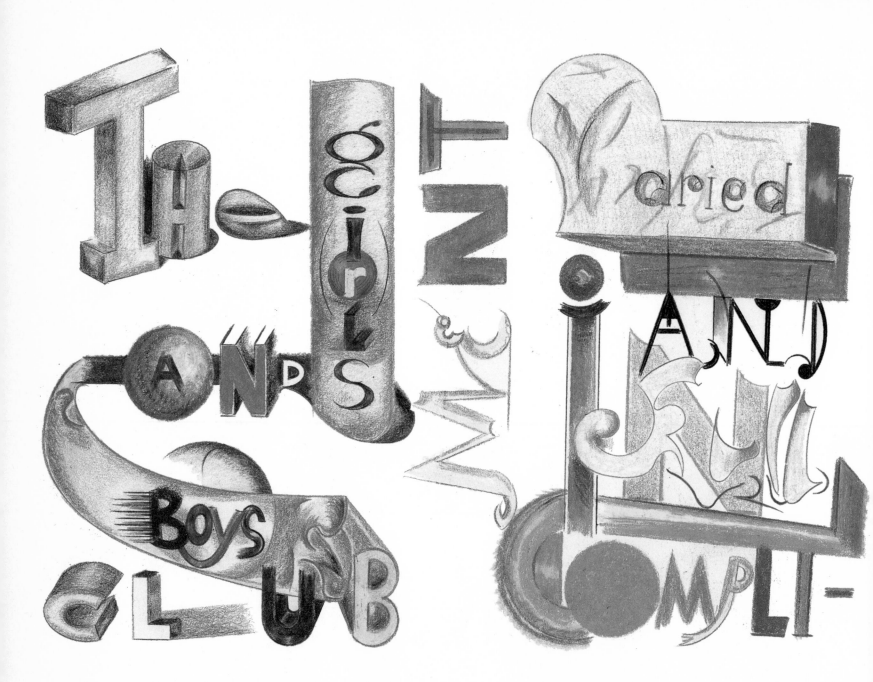

Fonts DEConfuse FUSE 2470 20-28 McBean Pkwy. Ppppppgggg BELGIUM

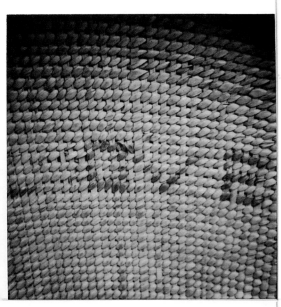

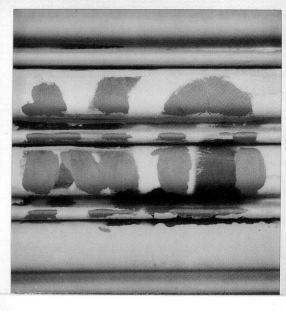

G I D I.N.C.
4 Q - 11 ZZ
L.I.C

M M CONT
116 KIMBAL A
YONKERS NY
10704

145 W 123 ST
N.Y 10024

MA SEA FO
54 GAN SEVOOR
NEW YORK N.Y

M.
HANIF
NTING & DECORAT
972·213

N.R.MARK
577 BROAD
N.Y, N Y,

J DIGGS
335 E 10
SEE
NYC

CBS NEWS
F J V
B'K L Y N
N. Y.

T C F
11 W. 52

GOURMET FOODS
IMPORTED
GLORIFIED GROCER
CIGARETTES
WINES
TEAS SPICES JELLIES JAMS
BEER
IMPORTED & DOMESTIC COFFEE
CHEESE

SHOPPER'S LIST
ICE-CREAM POP CHIPS
MAGAZINES
FILM / PHOTO SUPPLIES
BE

Black Spruce Wood Designs
East Hill FARM
Hugh Moss BIRD CARVINGS
The Red Door Collection

DRAPERY & CURTAIN CLEANING
EXPERT TAILORING & ALTERATIONS
SUEDE & LEATHER

APE CO
APE CO
APE CO

298-4011 298-4012
USED + NEW BOOKS
SPECIAL ORDER
LIVE PERFORMANCES

hauser
OBSTER PO
FISH MARK
COLD BEER & WINE
SIR CRICKET Fish'n'Chips FRIED CLAMS

MARKET
Collection
BIRD VINGS
ARM
NorthBound Books
Laris DESIGNS
Up North Casuals
CAUGHTAGE LIMITED Originals FURNITURE
The Good Earth
Black Horse Antiques

DOUBLE DRAGON
the Boardwalk
ON THE COVE
Nature Art
SHEARLOCKS HAIRSTYLING

Z SODA | 50¢

pecial — special — special
APPLE 1.00   16 oz
nly 1.00
NA 1.00   1.35   24 oz
special — special
IC 1.00   16 oz   1.35   24 oz
special — special
N SPRAY 1.00

L'Escargot a la
Salade Niço
Tian de Legu
Salade folle ....

LOTUS ICE
RED BEAN ICE
PINEAPPLE
DRAGON FRUIT
LYCHEE ICE
WATERMELON
LEMON ICE
ORANGE JUICE

ACON or HAM   1.50
S ON A ROLL   2.00
CON or HAM   1.75
    2.25
PLATTER with Home Fries & Toast 4.00
ON or HAM   4.50
    2.75

RB'S PUSHCA
OT DOGS
ANDWICHES
OUGHNUTS
UFFINS
OFEEE, HOT CH
ODAS, JUICES
ANDY

ablow	malo
abrahami	matisse
agrafiotis	melone
ali	moreh
aron	nagano
aronson	picasso
bak	pinardi
bezanson	rubin
braque	schantz
brauer	sharir
chagall	silber

TACOS DE
ADA, TRIPA, CARNITA
ASTOR, CABEZA, BUCHE
SOPES DE *
OLLO, ASADA, PASTOR
TORTAS DE ~~~?
ADA, PASTOR, CARNITAS
OSTADAS DE ~~~

BAKERY SPECIA
PPLE UPSIDE DOWN CAKE — $2.
N LOAF — $2.
E HORSE SHOE — $3.
H SODA BREAD — $1.9
IC BREAD — $1.2
T RAISIN BAGUETTE — $1.4
ZEL BAGUETTE — $1.2
ND ITALIAN — $1.00
T FREE/SUGAR FREE MUFFIN

THE SHOW IS O
VER   THE AUD
IENCE GET   UP
TO LEAVE THE
IR SEATS   TI
ME TO COLLECT
THEIR COATS
ND   GO HOM
HEY TURN   A

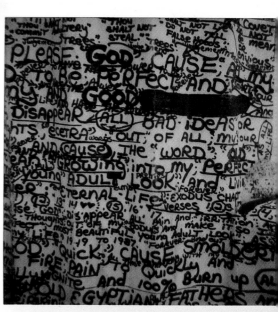

You'll See U CLA?

Valencia.

ZIP CODE 91355 85

.Design 'n' LETTERING

:HOT & NOT

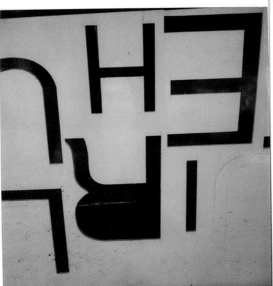

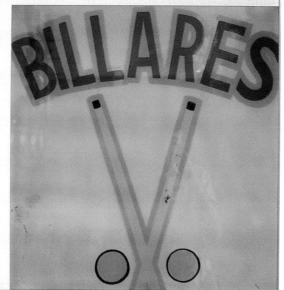

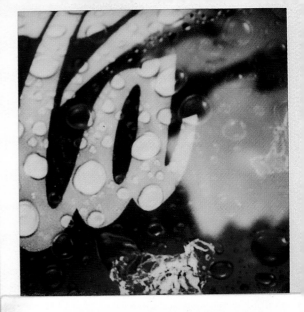

PUNCH 50th BIRTHDAY LAS VEGAS MAGNIFICENT X gifts PLS.

SLIDE LECTURE ON [A]

CALIFORNIA INSTITUT
F OF THE ARTS, SCHOOL
OF ART 27400 McBEA
N PKWY, VALENCIA CALI
F. 91355 (805) 255-1050

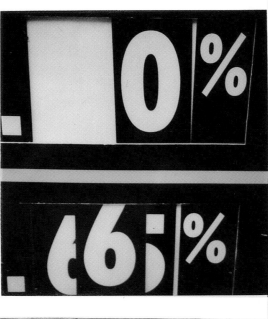

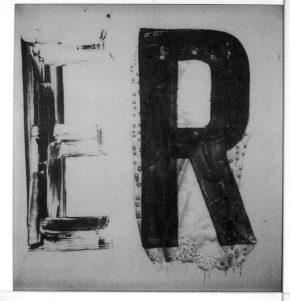

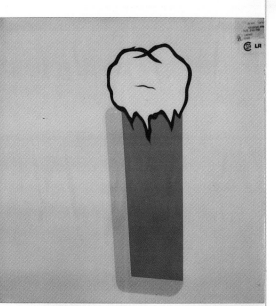

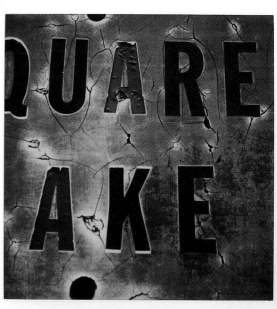

Award Winning 1999 *Central Nebraska Ethnic Festival* DOWNTOWN GRAND ISLAND, NEBRASKA

PUSH

CLOSE *Please Call A...*

Mien Mien oria

WHI W

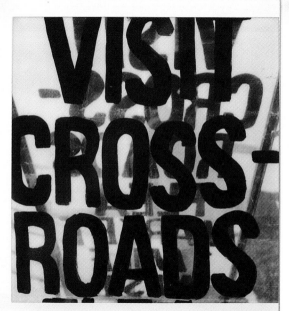

WILL BE 5 28TH ST EN PARK AND LEXINGTON Chairs Re

VISI CROSS- ROADS

HE WANT

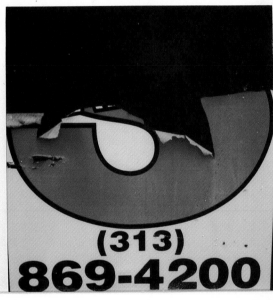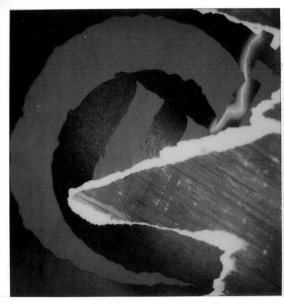
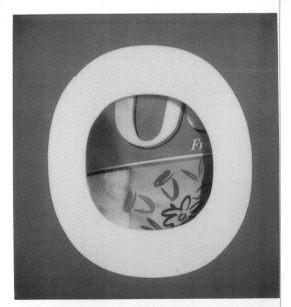

Cast Beyond the Surp-Line Othe

PROGRESSO SO SO SO SO SO.

CLARKSTON, MICHIGAN
Reception:
743 Beaubien
DETROIT, MI 48226
A GREAT EXTENT
UNIVERSITY
tel. 313 962~9025
On Monday.

CUBE
ICE

SE REPARAN
REFRIGERADORES
A
DOMICILIO
TEL 84-56-76

ATILDA
CAFE
123 E 4th
MEXICAN
FOOD

WATER
SKI
SHOW
VERY THUR 7PM

Diesel
ull Ser

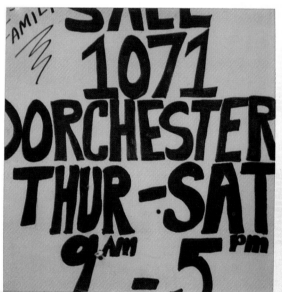

SALE
1071
DORCHESTER
THUR - SAT
9 AM - 5 PM

ITALIAN
ICECREAM

WE SELL
AIR
CONDITION

B & L
FEEDS

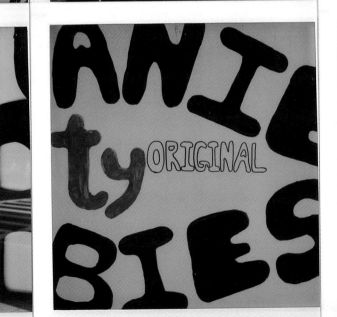

it's
already
sorted.
everything
in this bag

NEW STUFF
DAILY
ALWAYS
DISCOUNTED

SPOR
CAFE

OBACCO
JACKS
OBACCO
JACKS

EUNICE
LIQUO
CHEES
NATURE'S
PANTR

Pecans

BeeT
ME!

FRESH
CARROT
JUICE

N.Y YOGA & SHIATSU

← TOY MUSEUM →
OPEN JULY - AUG
WED, THURS, FRI, SAT

SODA'S MACHINE WORKING .75

ALL Childrens wear
50% Off

GHARC

STiTCH 552 105 TIME

SSPORT
* * 2/$6.99 + TAX
WHILE-U-WAI
PHOTO

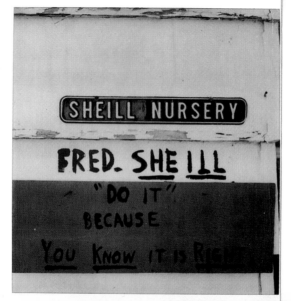

SHEILL NURSERY
FRED. SHE ILL
"DO IT" BECAUSE
YOU KNOW IT IS RIGHT

A STITCH N TIME 552 1053

Please Pay
At
BOOTH

RD-SALE
74 BANCRO
1ST
APTS

LA PLAYITA SEAFOOD
SUPER FUFFE
MEXICANO
Y
ENSALADA BAR
TODO LO QUE PUEDA
COMER

PEN 7-L
ATERMELO
MICH. TOMAT

aZWhimsy
& GIFTS

SHIPPING

·PEACHES·
-N-
·CREAM·

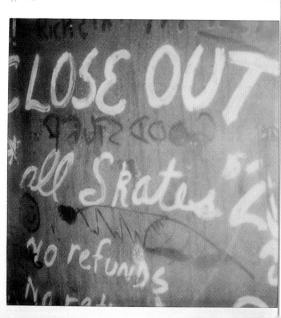

CLOSE OUT
all Skates 5.
no refunds

ICARUS
THE RETURN OF

BASEMENT
SALE
119, 8TH. ST.

JUNE 15TH & 16TH
7AM — 12 noon

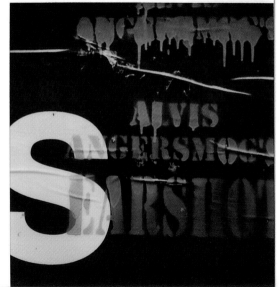

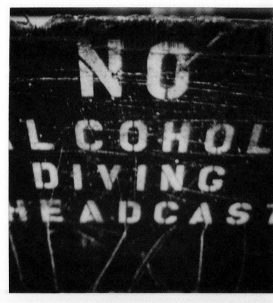

STEPHANIE
PSYCHIC
GALLERY
PALM TAROT
THE MAGIC
CARDS

1216
BEAUBIEN

ACE IS THE PLACE

SALE
GAS GRILLS
FANS
TRASH CANS

The Place
CAFE BAR
MINI MART
STRICH BURGERS
RESTROOMS

MANSION
STORIC ROOMS - SUITES
IIIPLACES

EAKFAST

DVENTUR
SED AQU
KAYAK
BIKES

PTIST CH
ALK IN
THE
LAW

SUNDAY SCH

ULKLEYS
AXIDERM
OPEN

POWERBA
ACKPOT $$
IT CASH $$
24 OZ FN
UNCH SPEC

10-45 PRELUDES
1:00 WORSHIP Se
Rev. ARLENE K.N
"You Are The C

POSTAGE
STAMP

For

RETURN
STICKER from

To ADDRESS
LABEL

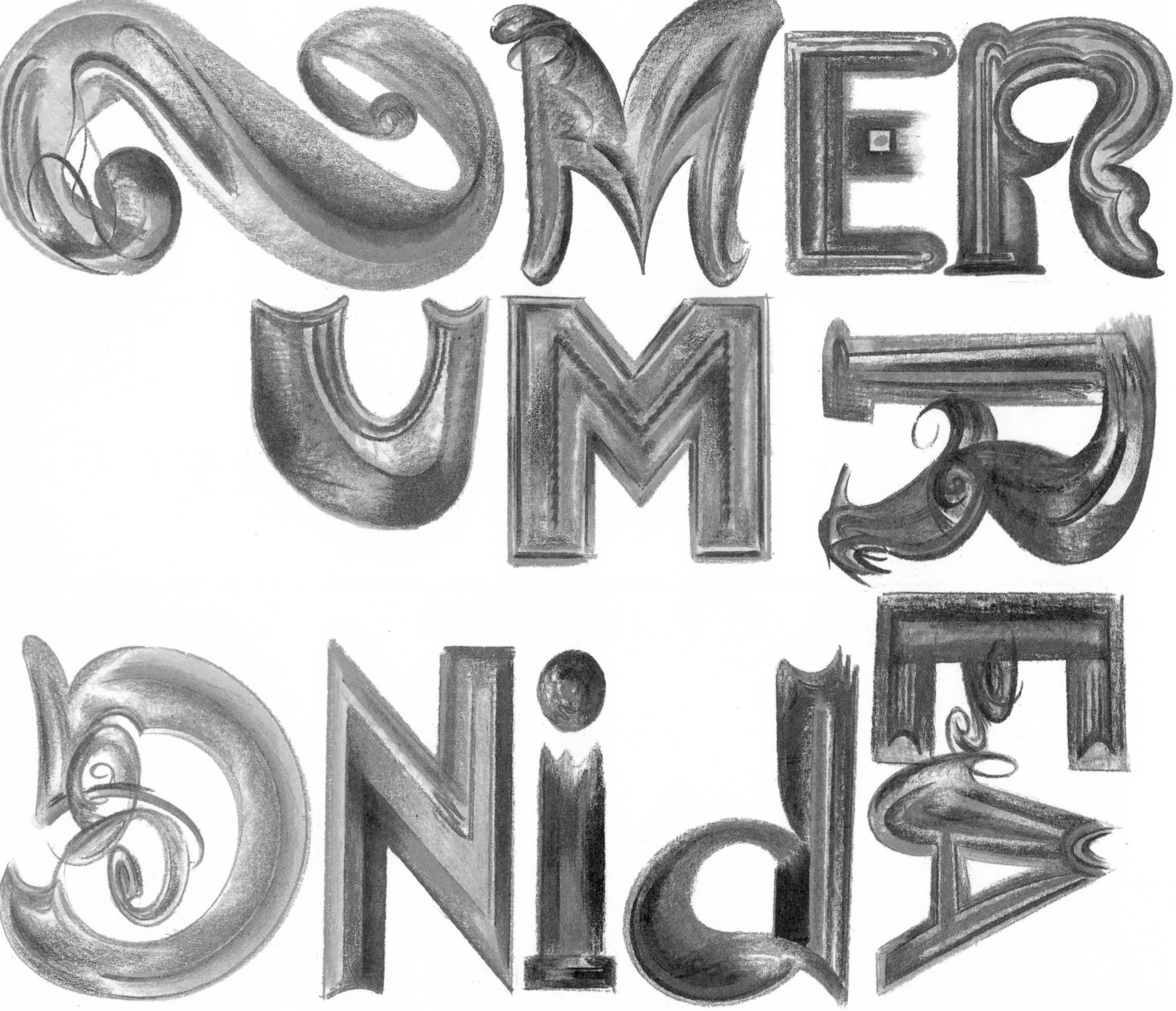

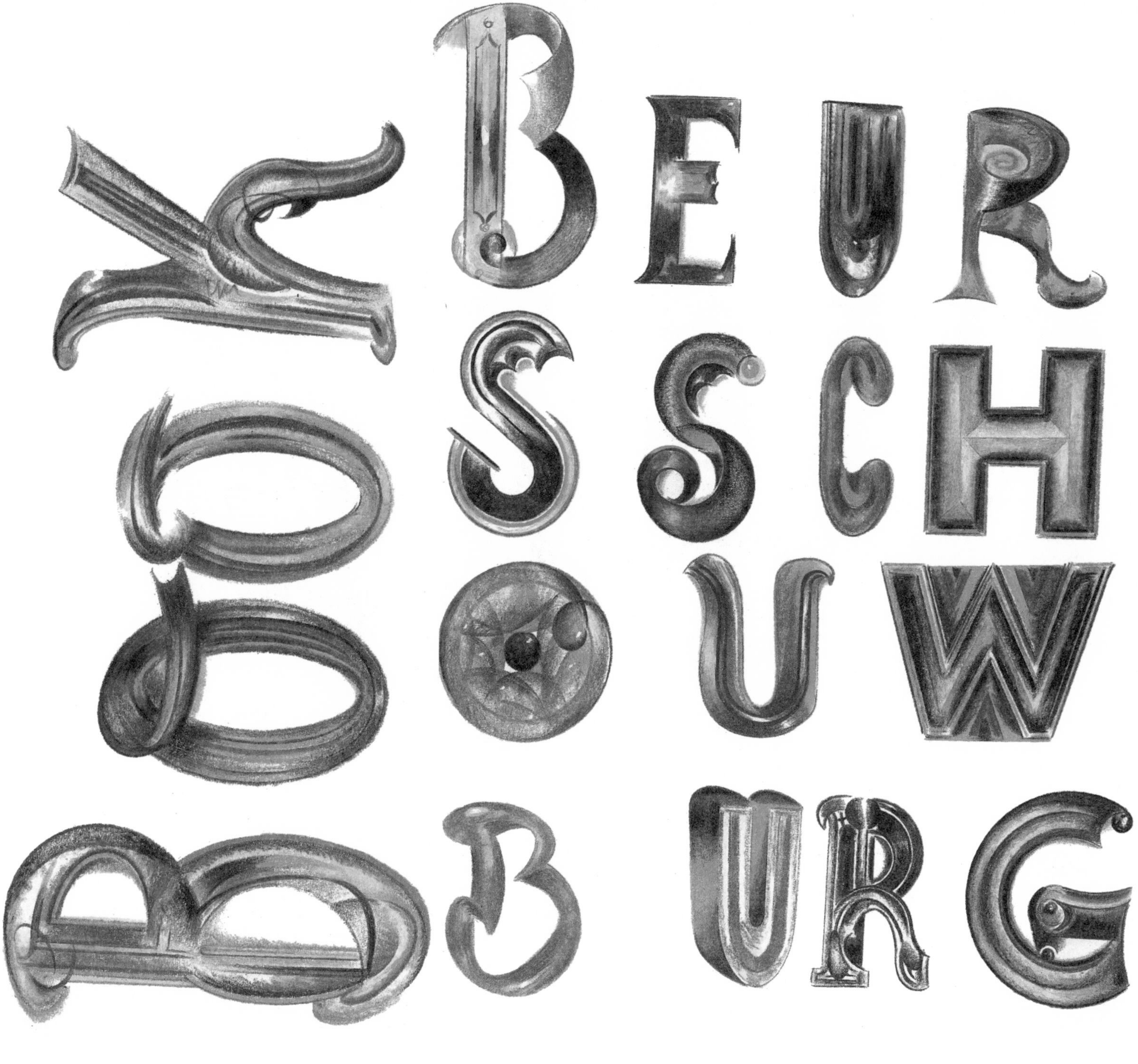
BOOK
BEURSSCHOUWBURG

Graphite ROD
S CHOOOOLOOF ART
Cult & Culture
8th OCT
ART CENTER
KLINKENDE

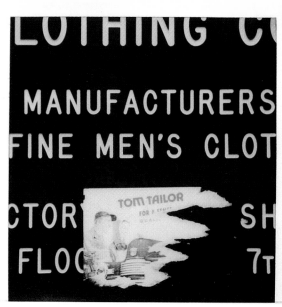

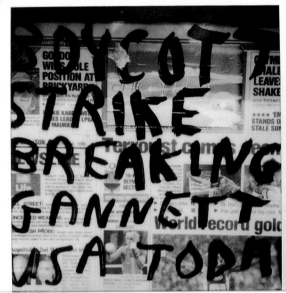

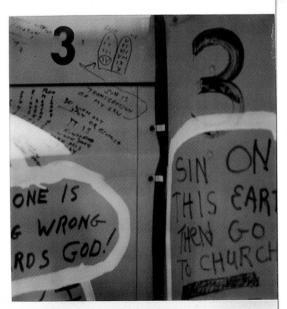

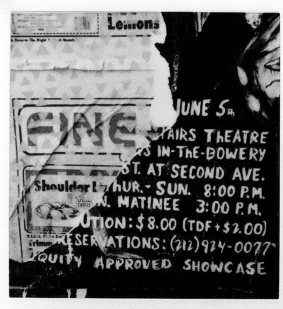

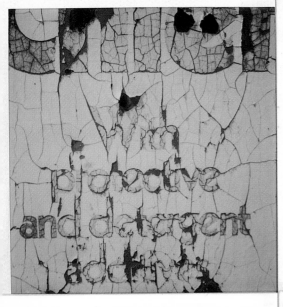
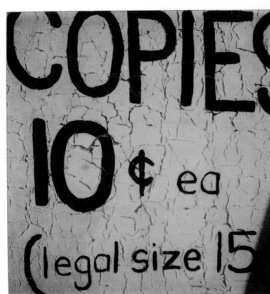

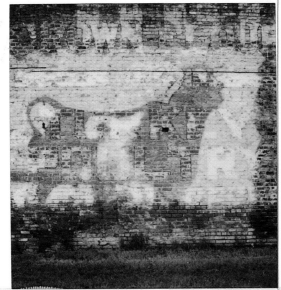

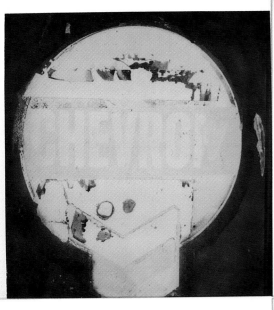

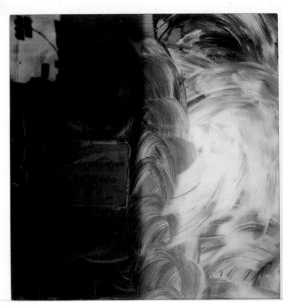

Annoy Toy

Buoy Ahoy Toy
Overjoy Toy
& Toy
Hoi Polloi Toy
Illinois Toy
Toy
Corduroy Employ To y
ToyToy.

LOS
ANGELES
CALIF.
CALIFORNIA

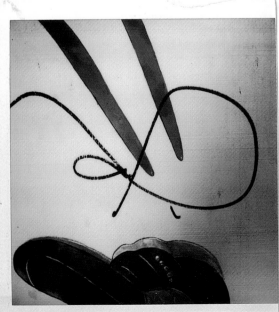

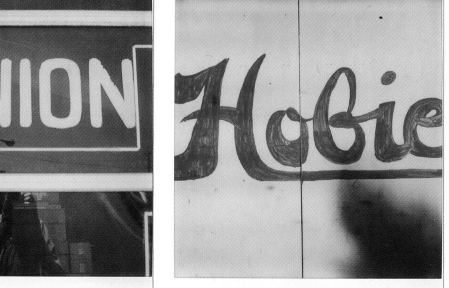

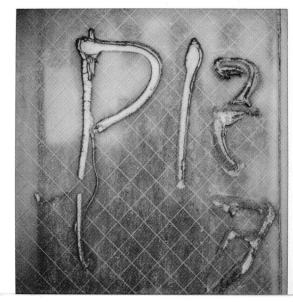

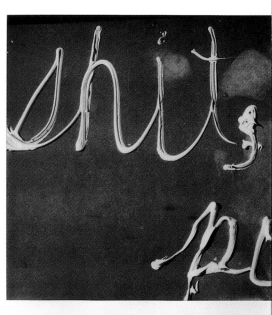

8 PIECE
CHICKEN
$?

STOP R...
enJoy
LiFe

PRECIPICE
SHOW
ESPRESSO

home &
acces

CLOVERIE
RESTAURANT
SERVING
BREAKFAST
STARTING 6 A.M.
ALL DAY
ART
FAIR

VEGI
HOT-DO
$.99

DELIVERIES
IN
REAR

ERM
$39.95!
Reg
55
COMPLETE

office
FoR
LEASE
CALL
75-2-9114

SALESGIRL
WANTED
INQUIRY
WITHIN

SHOE
REPAIR

HOT
RESH GO
COFF

LA
TIENDA
GARCIA

THURS & SAT ~ 8:00 ~ to
FRI ~ 8:00 to 6:3
AY ~ 8:00 to ~ 4:00

Critical
Studies

OLD
DRINKS
AILABLE 00

AIR
Condition

SPECIAL SALE
O
CARROT JUICE

carrot, Beet & apple & Ginger
carrot, apple, Beet,

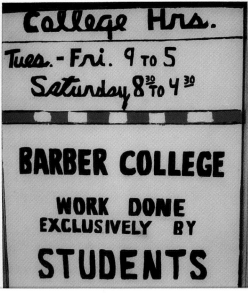
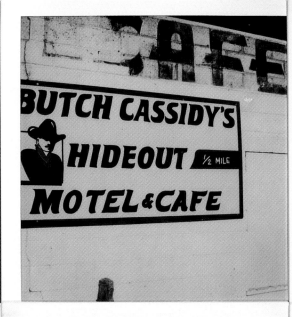

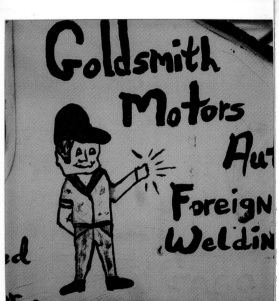

Artistry
OF HAIR...

REPLACEMENT & WEAVING CENTER

542-2368
542-2367

Barber

WOME
LDREN
N NOW
34-7065

BELT A...

A BREAK
THE OLDEST
CH IN HYANNIS
1771   7-8:30
he door is open to all
> THUR-FRI-S

WEAR
infants to size 7
girls size 7~14
GIFT ITEMS
BEDDING
LAYETTE
ACCESSORIES

Simón Sih

Will Be
SIGNING
FROM
12:00 - 6:00

LIBERY ST.
VIDEO
Will be
CLOSED
ON

BREAKFAST
ROOMS A D SUITES
WITH FIREPLACES
VICTORIAN FAMILY HO
FREE TOURS

The Pantry
atural Food
~and~
Supplements
e Tabor St. in rec

- grading
- driveways
- corrals clean
- Snow plowed
Fence Work
646-3777

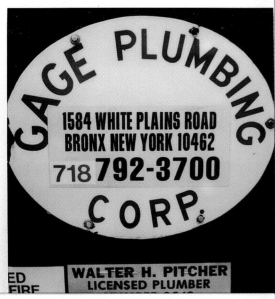

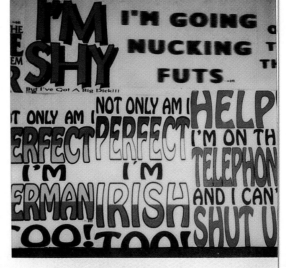

JAPANESE & OTHER
ORIENTAL DELICACIES

LUNCH & DINNER
EAT•IN OR TAKE•OUT
PER DISH $1.99 & UP

SUSHI   SASHIMI
SUKIYAKI   TEMPURA
NOODLES   VEGETABLE

ORGANIC VEGETARIAN
HOT FOOD BAR
NO MSG

JUICE BAR

AND

OUR LEASE
BY OWNER: 924-5?
ERYTHI
MUST GO

"CAR-
"NUT -WO L
ED-TAIL.
E GIVE WASH
AX. $48
*   N WASH

CTS
34 5 7?
BRK N

CHUBBY MONDA
ALL-U-CAN EAT   PINTS
$14.95 $3
WINGS   NACHO
$3 $3
ROZEN $3   DRINK

ADULT • $2.00
BOAT $2.00
CAMPING $2.00
ELECT. $7.00

RON AND TENANT P
RS: PATRONS - 10 AM T
TENANTS - UNRESTR
RATE — $5.00
290 NORTHERN AVE BOSTO
TEL. 542-7770
C.NO. 53 • CAP.9 3PA
TENANT

NEW YORK
PIZZARIA
PIZZA & PASTA
GRINDERS
795·2424   795·2425

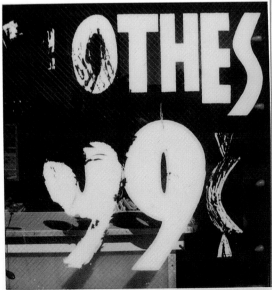

OLITA
WEEK-END
YTHING
$¢
¢

WILL
VACATiON
JULY 22
. 6.
THANK YOU.

LDO DE
ES
4.75
+tax

SPECIAL
HOT Co
Fresh Salad 2

EVERYDAY
LOW
PRICES

Spoo
and
Co
CAVE TOURS
0 MILES WEST

.M. TO 6 F
MMERCIAL VEHICL
USE PERMIT EXE
ONDAY ON
CITY OF LOS

PLEASE
RING BELL

LAUNDRY: W
$-
CHEAPEST DRY CLEANING

COMING
OR
GOING

T O P
N RED
GNAL

N P
STER ST
Y.C.

TOYNBEE IDEAS
IN KUBRICK:200|
RESURRECT DEA|
ON PLANET JUPITER

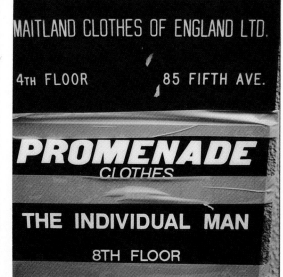

MAITLAND CLOTHES OF ENGLAND LTD.

4TH FLOOR   85 FIFTH AVE.

PROMENADE
CLOTHES

THE INDIVIDUAL MAN

8TH FLOOR

A C T I V E
D O O R

24   HR.

Dinner
6:00 p.m

PAINTS
ES & SERV
ay·Betty Nieu
G   SAL
AND SER

ITs A
BoY!
JESSE JOHN
ROSE
NIOXIN®
AVAILABLE HERE!

Notes on Edward Fella: Design in a Border Town (1991)

by Lorraine Wild

1.

(from a description of Giulio Camillo of Venice, who, in the 1530's was attempting to build a 'memory theatre' which would hold signs of all existing knowledge in the world)

'The work is of wood, marked with many images, and full of little boxes; there are various orders and grades in it. He gives a place to each individual figure and ornament…he stammers badly and speaks Latin with difficulty, excusing himself with the pretext that through continually using his pen he has nearly lost the use of speech. He is said however to be good in the vernacular…'[1.]

Has that much ever really been said about the incredible scavenging that shadows commercial art practice? The miles of 'clip files', the piles of reference books, the endless gobbling up of magazines, the flea-marketing, the insatiable collection of ephemera? This mania surfaces every once in a while, for instance, during the recent public revelation that an illustrator of a *TV Guide* cover had collaged Oprah Winfrey's head on Ann Margaret's body…because Ann Margaret's body had on just the right outfit. To anyone acquainted with common illustration methods this episode implied that the exposed illustrator had probably collected a universe of dressy torsos in some file folder, just in case the right assignment came along – and sure enough, it did.

To understand Edward Fella's work one has to recognize the age-old project undertaken by so many artists, writers and thinkers: collecting, reordering and re-stating everything about the surrounding culture that can be observed and remembered, thereby laying claim to (one's own interpretation of) the universe.

There's a didactic, crackpot edge to the classifying impulse to 'get it right' or 'set the record straight' but in the process of creating a new canon or catalogue, the talented ones end up defining themselves and creating that new culture, by and by.

For Edward Fella the starting point of his catalogue was the towering pile of any illustrator's reference material: the books, the photos, the lettering guides, the type books, old post-cards, clip files and a mental encyclopedia of visual style, all of it just in case. True, he did mix some peculiar things into the investigation: way too much interest in higher forms of art, literature and cultural history than can be explained by his high-school trade education, or by the environment of the commercial art studios in Detroit that he worked in so diligently and successfully for the first fifteen years of his design-life.

2.

(a quote Fella repeats in three different sketchbooks)
'This "I" which approaches the text is already itself a plurality of other texts…
  (EF notes: it's what you already know (too much!)
of codes which are infinite or, more precisely, lost (whose origin is lost'). — Roland Barthes

The path of Edward Fella's work spirals out from inside the conventions of commercial art/design, to its borderlines—and then stops just at the edges, or straddles the fence between whatever separates design from something else (and many think his work is just beyond the pale). Far from being a 'hand' (an illustrator that can mimic any number of styles), Edward Fella's illustration originally consisted mainly of pen-and-ink line drawings which were referred to as 'cartoons', not in the comic book and animation sense, but in the older definition of the cartoon as a sort of caricature, a visual skewering. Inflexibility of style and media was more than compensated for by wit and humour. Fella's mordant drawings poked fun at all types of human type and endeavour, and (when the assignment was decorative borders or headlines) at typography, too. Although he received a fair share of awards and recognition from commercial work, it was always considered by his peers to be somewhat eccentric: he claimed that the strangeness in his work stemmed from desperate attempts to circumvent the limits of his 'hand'. He developed a fast, funny and perfectly executed commercial product. It was not for nothing that his fellow illustrators jokingly referred to him as 'the king of zing'.

The decorative illustration had real impact on what was to follow. Fella's preferred lettering style was a parody of Art Deco faces that he called 'shiny shoe' or 'cleaners' modern' in reference to the style of many Depression-era laundries built in and around Detroit. This ornate stuff was constructed by hand with circle guides and triangles, and was in no way an accurate reproduction of anything seen during the twenties, but like the rest of his caricature, it got at the essential nature of the original lettering that was laughable but dead-on. He did the same with hand-scrawled versions of Victorian flourishes, and parodies of other vernaculars as well. Years later, while pursuing a graduate school education (quite removed from the commercial art business), he began to confront the typography of high design culture—and his approach was completely consistent. Fella's deep structure is embedded in those illustrator's reference files, and the files are horizontal, not hierarchical—so high design was just more stylistic grist for his mill, to personalize by 'getting it wrong'. Many graphic designers look at Edward Fella's work and, unable to see anything but error, cannot believe that it is there by design. But that only indicates the severity of the split between 'high' art, 'mid' design culture and 'low' commercial art culture. One of the many ironies about the current fascination with the synthesis of high and pop cultures that allegedly marks our age is the fact that work which truly challenges the classifications is still met with great difficulty, particularly if it emanates from the mid-range of design—and this is the story of Edward Fella's project.

3.

(from a clipping in one of Ed's sketchbooks)
 'Dear Ann Landers: I am 17 years old and want more than anything in the world to be an artist. The few people who have been shown my work discouraged me by saying I'm not "with it." Any advice?   — Downbeat in Torrance
    Dear T.: Take heart in the words of Orson Welles. He said, "I passionately hate the idea of being 'with it'. A true artist is always out of step with his time. He has to be."'
(Ed adds comment: 'Another great popular cult of art myth').

By the early seventies, art had been made out of a lot of things, including neon tubes, and very big holes bulldozed out of the earth (and of course urinals and snow-shovels); it wasn't until ten years later that it would be made out of type and large halftoned photostats. Pop-art made commercial art into a subject for painting, which was obliquely flattering to commercial artists but which absolutely did not include them. (Author's note: the wall between graphic design and commercial art is dwarfed by the wall separating all of it from art. For instance: at least some graphic designers keep up with *Art in America*, *Artforum*, etc. How many 'real' artists do you think will see this issue of *Emigre*?) Fella's Bauhaus-influenced education taught him to idealize a combination of art and design practice; but still, art was painting and that was something he only got to do on weekends. As art de-materialized in the seventies it remained difficult to integrate as a motif into promotions for car dealerships and florists and banks and other typical clients. Fella turned to marginal art practices, especially photography, to augment his work. It helped that photography was pictorial, but it was not the pictures that became his subject matter. It was the detail of seeing, the little conceptual moves that turned the act of photographing from a banal procedure to a vehicle for meaning and a work of art that became so interesting. Ed Rusha, Andy Warhol, Robert Frank, Lee Friedlander, 'artist's books', folk art, 'mall' art and flea-market antiques—all were added to Fella's frame of reference, and it was at this point that the edges began to blur.

Staff illustrators in design studios have lots of down time between assignments, and Edward Fella used his the way most illustrators do, to make 'samples'. These are comps of imaginary projects meant to demonstrate one's capabilities in a way that printed samples did not, which a salesman would take to show to potential clients, which might bring about a real job where the experiment could be put to use. When not cartooning, Fella used samples to tread into art territory. In 1974, he used his studio's first direct-positive photostat system to produce a book of collages instantly composed of found imagery and type. He had always made collages, but now because of the stats, they were easy to translate into graphic media. The pages are based on the genre of magazine design (where most of the imagery came from) but the sparse juxtaposition of images and tiny bits of type is like a caricature of the minimalism of late Swiss corporate design. However, the content, which is mostly cryptic, contradicts the clarity of the style. It is all wrong, which leads you to inspect individual elements more carefully. Suddenly everything is 'strange' ('Nothing is more fantastic ultimately than precision').[2] What Fella had ingested from art and photography—an obsession with process, art defined not by an identifiable visual style but by a series of intellectual moves in space and time—was conflated with the puns and pop images of commercialism in his new sample book—and it did not yield him any commissions. But it set him permanently on the course that led to his current work. It also had a large impact on the design programme that the McCoys were setting up at Cranbrook, just a few miles away. Fella would show his experimental work to the students (a more appreciative audience than his art business peers) and his scavenging of art and design became a model for much work produced there. From the McCoys and Cranbrook, he developed a more refined appreciation for the rational methodology of design: you see him synthesize it with his old caricaturing mode in a series of rigorous but intuitively 'friendly' symbols designed for several departments of Detroit's Henry Ford Hospital. The programme is straight out of any corporate manual but the visual style is a funny rendition of stencilled images, completely unlike the geometric visual language of the typical institutional identity system.

4.

(from a 1984 sketchbook)
 'I force myself into Self-Contradiction to avoid following
 my own taste'   —Marcel Duchamp

Between the time that Edward Fella began to produce his hybrid art/design work (which could be interpreted as art about design,

in materials not usually encountered in anything recognized as art, at least fifteen years ago) and the next ten years or so, when he gradually pulled out of commercial practice to concentrate on his own education, he began to work with a variety of alternative arts organizations in Detroit—The Detroit Focus Gallery, The Poetry Resource Center, The Detroit Artists Market. He began to produce printed materials for openings, announcements, temporary signs, small catalogues—all of it extremely low-budget, but free of constraint. Through his work in the 'samples', then a set of xeroxed collages and little books, and finally a set of sketchbooks, he had wandered even farther into terra incognita of the professional graphic designer—but the work was still 'design', it was made up of type and photographs and arranged clearly. Fella's work was always 'legible', but not in the completely linear way most design is. For a designer like Fella, who had been used to working with professional suppliers paid by big production budgets, stepping down to the erratic quality of cheap typesetting and 'quickie' offset printing was a radical move, but one that he had to make (since it was all the organizations could afford) in order to see the experiments of his collages and sketchbooks realized. He slowly built an audience out of the Detroit arts community – and eventually they took him as seriously as he took them.

Fella claims that he could never figure out how to modulate his experimental work into the routine commercial design and illustration projects that he produced, that he was only able to flourish when he had complete control over the projects for the arts organizations. But in that work he did develop hierarchies of experimentation which imitate the range of possible in 'real' work. For instance, the *Detroit Focus Quarterly* is typographically conservative, true to the genre of art publications; but there are visual puns and buried themes in photo choices (for instance, everyone will be posed similarly, etc.) that are not too blatant but can be appreciated upon closer inspection. In a series of posters for photography exhibitions, an angle of vision or composition will be echoed in the ostensibly minimal typography; in the case of the Rauhauser poster, typographic detail from the image of the Leica is integrated into what appears to be quite normal, tasteful art typography. It is usually considered to be very bad form for graphic design to provide anything but the most reverential, neutral frame when the subject is *Art*. But Fella insists on intervening with the subject. In 1987, he produced two remarkable catalogues: one on the work of Morris Brose (published by the Detroit Arts Market) and the other for an exhibition of the work of Phillip Fike and Bill Rauhauser at the Detroit Focus Gallery. In the Brose catalogue, big chunks of type move muscularly across the pages, mimicking the weight and gravity of Brose's work. Photographs are cropped in extreme shapes that induce a visual anxiety by emulating the formal strategy of Brose's sculpture in the 'wrong' media.

In the Fike/Rauhauser catalogue, photographs of the artists are embellished with shapes that Fella has added, which seem disconnected from their work. The presence of the designer is noted more aggressively than custom ever allows, and design as one of the many invisible support systems in the art world is highlighted with a vengeance.

5.

(EF sketchbook. Nov. 1985)
'Tell the truth but tell it slant/Success in Circuit lies'
—Emily Dickinson

Now Edward Fella is a faculty member in the graphic design programme at the California Institute of the Arts (CalArts), where he works with fourth year and graduate students. He keeps designing Detroit Focus announcements (by overnight mail) and he diligently produces sketchbook after sketchbook of drawings and collages; these two projects are the main 'lab' where Fella keeps performing his new experiments. (Fella is an unusual teacher; he possesses decades of experience but he rejects it as a source of authority since he is almost entirely involved with speculation.)

There are not many precedents for Fella's position in graphic design now. He produces work that, because of its media, scale and audience, is usually called graphic design, but which flaunts the professional conventions of it. Rotten work is nothing new, since it is more often done, knowingly or unknowingly, by printers, artists or anyone with access to 'desktop publishing'—but Fella toys with the border between what is acceptable and what is not from deep within the establishment, his own history of thirty-some years of design practice, and a graduate education from Cranbrook. He cannot be accused of any sort of naivety.

The first position Fella takes, which can only make many designers wince, is to declare that his formal experimentation is purely in the service of his own aesthetic gratification and nothing else. (This of course is not quite true, or we would not be looking at his work right now—but that is his cross to bear.) Fella proceeds from the point that all standards (particularly typographic ones that imply a kind of mastery of expertise) are not necessarily wrong, but in his particular case, irrelevant. He refuses to find the solution in the problem (a great design cliché if ever there was one): in fact, conveying a message is never a problem in his work—messages are usually as clear as bells. But he does concoct enormous problems by upsetting every rule associated with functional typography (while remaining completely cognizant that design is defined in part by its 'obedience' to a highly mutable set of standards of public tastes).

For instance: how easy is it to compose a page using only typefaces whose names rhyme? What new aesthetic emanates from that small, strange decision? He is not trying to perfect an old style or invent a new one: all situations are unique and deserving of a whole new approach. It is this quality which is so relevant to the kinds of design now possible on the computer. Even though his work is painstakingly created by hand, it is a model of complexity that is really only viable on the computer. Fella talks about looking for crude archetypes for lettering, and while many designers have appreciated the vitality of amateur lettering, few have had the nerve to actually incorporate its characteristics into their work. While a graduate student at Cranbrook, he began by taking photostats of existing faces and 'adjusting' them by slicing serifs or strokes with his X-acto knife. He has continued to do this, guided by a set of formal precepts which celebrate discordant or unbalanced elements; irregularities of shape, letter- and word-spacing; ambivalent base-lines; and almost imperceptible degrees of contrast rendered by types of slightly different weight. Fella's own standards of 'similar differences' or 'inconsistent irregularities' are in direct opposition to the simplified notions of contrast inherited from modernist typography (as articulated by Moholy-Nagy and Tschichold) but again are much more reflective of the plasticity made possible in contemporary computerized typesetting. So, although he has avoided the computer so far, his work does address the complete and total technological change sweeping over typography today. It has been noted that the grand technological change that we are now witnessing has to have some impact on the aesthetic principles of design: perhaps Edward Fella's work is demonstrating what those shifts might be?

But to look at his work only for that is to distort what it really is, which cannot possibly be described in its entirety, because like Camillo's Memory Theatre, it contains so many bits and pieces, quotations and signs, organized in such a personal manner, that it can't really all be rationalized. In the flyers for exhibitions at the Detroit Focus Gallery, all sorts of elements and techniques are catalogued, sometimes in reference to the subject, sometimes so obliquely that the joke just lies there, waiting for some astute observer. He reserves the prerogative to interact with the artists, or to stage a sideshow. A very subtle example of this is his design for the 10th Anniversary catalogue for the Detroit Focus Gallery. Its style is typical of the sort of conventionally subdued form that design takes when the subject is an art institution. But the entire 80-page book is pasted up by hand without tools, columns of type and blocks of photographs simply 'eyeballed' as if there is a grid; but of course it wobbles, ever so slightly. From the design, you could infer that the presence of this alternative institution has positively destabilized the more closed cultural milieu which existed before its history; or you could infer that the institution is flaunting its own flexibility, or perhaps admitting that it exists on shaky ground. Or, if you are not prone to close-reading, you could simply miss the whole thing!

6.

(EF, 1986)
'finger on exactly identifying that meddlesome art touch in the design pie...'

In many of the real professions whose status is envied by the quasi-profession of design, there is a very clear distinction made between levels and genres of practice. The neighbourhood no-fault divorce lawyer is different from the academic specialist, and they in turn are different than the highly-paid corporate counsel or the idealistic public defender. But genres of graphic design practice are rarely distinguished from each other and therefore the common assumption is that all design has to rest upon a set of shared 'values' which are mostly based on style and production quality. Look at any edition of *Print's Regional Annual*—there is no perceptible difference between the work that is chosen from different parts of the country, because the representatives of the profession that curate the work would tend *not* to recognize anything that falls outside of this very generalized set of specifications as being graphic design at all. This delusion stems from the time not so long ago when self-conscious graphic design was produced by a small group of modernist initiates. Some nostalgic designers (mostly over 50) are somewhat bitter about its passing, dismayed by the hordes of young designers and the (inadvertent) loss of production control brought on by the new technology. Edward Fella, 53, continues to play in his self-defined 'border town' of design practice (declared in the border town of Detroit, unconcerned with the mainstream of either one of the Coasts), surrounded by the piles of clip files, books, type samples, art magazines, novels, Polaroids that he has been trying to make sense out of for thirty years. It is in Fella's style to discount the work, to insist that it is all for fun and without consequence, and maybe he has to maintain that line in order to be able to continue to produce it when it is not recognized by many as being art or design. But there are many who appreciate his work for the tough questions implied by its very existence. Can graphic designers ever really be accepted as anything other than obedient mediums lubricating the messages of their clients? Is there any room in the transmission of messages for the designer's static? Could friction be a vital element in 'problem solving'? Are designers really smart enough and creative enough to be able to see the opportunity to take a more aggressive role in their work? Can work that is produced for practically nothing be taken seriously in our slick profession, or is a budget (and a map) now attached to the definition of design? Can design that embraces the culture of design as subject matter, be understood by other designers without them becoming defensive ('oh, that's just design about design!') and fearful, or must designers wander about in a state of perpetual ingenuousness? Must design always be *put to work?* Edward Fella doesn't presume to have the answers, but he just keeps rephrasing the question in a million permutations, just in case.

endnotes

1. Francis Yates, *The Art of Memory*. University of Chicago Press, Chicago, 1966. Pg. 13

2. Robbe-Grillet, quoted in John Hejduk, *Mask of Medusa*. Rizzoli International Publications, New York, 1985. Pg. 39

Postscript, 2000

by Lorraine Wild

In this book, on the pages of uncoated paper wedged between the grids of Polaroid photographs, are pages of lettering drawn by Edward Fella. These pages show fragments of his lettering from earlier projects that have been reproduced on flyers and announcements and a few commercial projects. The pages have been arranged to make visual compositions without regard to meaning. In their original sources, the fragments combine (with other fragments not shown here) to form complete messages; but in these pages they appear without their original contexts. In that sense, they are similar to the fragments of lettering that are the subject of the Polaroids, since in the majority of those pictures one sees only fragments of messages, as well.

In both the photographs and the pages of lettering fragments, the lack of a complete message forces the viewer to concentrate on what is there: an intense observation of the vagaries of form of letters (in the case of the Polaroids), 'found' as Edward Fella sees them, and (in the case of the lettering pages), drawn as (only) Fella draws them. There's an intricate relationship between the lettering and the photographs that is very important yet less direct than the viewer might imagine.

The drawn fragments of lettering may be divorced from their original situations, but the new context created here (by juxtaposing the fragments against the Polaroids) creates a new opportunity for understanding Fella's lettering.

There is the cliché about Fella that his work is all about the vernacular. The issue of 'the vernacular' as it has been used and abused by graphic designers, particularly during the last decade, is a complicated one — especially the question of which narrow range of vernaculars are quoted (or more frequently, knocked-off) and what is really gained by contemporary designers (and their audiences) through varying degrees of mimicry. Fella's photographs document several vernaculars. All of the lettering he shoots falls into the broad category of the commercial — signs, public notices, announcements. The photographs are all taken out in the commercial world of the street, the shop-window, the telephone pole, etc. None of the pictures are shot from books or previously published sources of lettering; and although some of them fit into that more picturesque thing that most designers think they know when they use the term 'vernacular', a lot of them would go absolutely unnoticed if it were not for Fella's careful discernment of worthy formal expression in so many tiny samples of the banal commercial environment.

Of course, when Edward Fella's lettering is placed next to the Polaroids of 'the real thing', the difference between the cataloguing of lettering fragments as a documentation of commercial lettering vernaculars — and the creation of a highly personal and synthetic lettering that is distanced from its vernacular sources — is demonstrated with a vengeance. Fella's lettering reveals itself as much more wildly synthetic and personal and original than any of the lettering that he documents: however, there are qualities of hand in the vernacular lettering that Fella would somewhat jealously admit he could never duplicate, much less invent.

In 'Design in a Border Town' I described Fella's practice, drawn on his training as an illustrator, to create 'clip files' and other extensive collections of visual material saved as raw data to use when necessary for reference. On the face of it, it seems that Fella's Polaroid documentation of vernacular lettering was created, at least initially, as an attempt to make a useful archive of lettering styles. Fella took lots and lots of other Polaroids too (he has hundreds of images documenting faces, for instance) but this category of the commercial lettering vernaculars was obviously propelled by personal interest in the drawing of letters.

However, the Polaroids were not really taken out of the same sort of necessity that propels an illustrator's clip file. Fella admits that once the photos are taken, he never gives them a second look. He claims that some of his motivation for taking the pictures in the first place was out of solidarity for the low-end of the commercial art business, an appreciation of the craft of the signpainter, an acknowledgement of kinship based on a shared background, pre-graphic design, of the craft of hand-lettering. Younger designers might appreciate the vernacular from an aesthetic or nostalgic distance, but he feels that he is much more directly connected to these anonymous graphic practitioners since he was schooled in the very same techniques they use. Typically self-deprecating, Fella says that the only real difference between his work and the lettering that he documents, is his own 'slickness' or 'artiness', qualities that he cannot shake since he knows too much, having travelled beyond the confines of that genre.

Fella's own lettering is all drawn by hand. His letters are not based on a knowledge of classical typography, the study of proportion and letterforms, or a typographic training derived from the older skills connected to the design of letterforms before digitalization. Instead, Fella's lettering is based on techniques to construct letters using drafting tools, stencils or Speedball pens. These techniques can all be found, explained and illustrated, in many self-instructional manuals on commercial lettering that Fella would have been exposed to during his study of commercial art at Cass Technical High School in Detroit in the mid-1950s. After that, he put these methods into practice as part of his work as an illustrator in advertising-oriented design studios in Detroit, drawing titles, headlines and phrases for use in magazines, brochures and the like. Fella produced the lettering with circle and ellipse guides and templates, a combination of rapidograph pen and coloured pencil, utilizing the basic hand-skills which were common to commercial designers and illustrators trained before the onset of digital production.

As always with Fella, necessity is the mother of invention: he based his hand-lettering on what he could do, minus the more refined skills of the specialized 'lettering men' who were still employed by design studios in Detroit until the cheaper proliferation of photo-lettering. Combining his limitations as a draughtsman with a sense of humour, Fella's early commercial lettering was mostly a caricature of the hard geometry of Art Deco, since that is the kind of form those tools render best. When Fella started producing lettering in the 1960s, the 1920s were considered humorously 'camp', and the bad taste of Art Deco worked with the sardonic nature of the illustration and cartoons for which he was infamous. Although it was designed decades later, Fella's font OutWest (published by Emigre in 1993) is a good example of how he utilized retro advertising lettering techniques with attitude and wit. In OutWest the construction of the letters of the alphabet (made entirely with ellipse guides) is the design, revealed in skeleton form, partially blacked in with ink in either of its 'Half Empty' or 'Half Full' versions.

Fella spent the seventies experimenting with composing pages of text spontaneously, through pasting-up photostated chunks of type in unorthodox, unaligned arrangements. In the mid-seventies he began to work in a continuous series of notebooks, some of which concentrated on the rendering of letters and phrases. Ten years later, when he was a graduate student in the design department at the Cranbrook Academy of Art, he began to produce work that utilized existing typefaces that he had 'customized' by altering them in minute but significant ways — shaving off serifs, for instance, or creating angles by either cutting into the letters or adding on to them. Fella would draw or manipulate the letters that he needed, photostat them, and then cut them up and use them as art for mechanicals. In fact, he did not regularly produce complete fonts, but the results looked like they came from complete fonts (since the manipulation was less obvious than in the completely hand-drawn letters). Many people assumed that the customization had been digitized somehow (in part because few could believe that Fella could tolerate the amount of hand-work that he did in order to create the rich variety of subtle effects 'the old-fashioned way'). The overall effect was an attack on the 'authority' of fonts themselves, which up to that point had been inviolate in either their hard-metal or fixed-photographic forms. Ironically, although Fella was making his work by hand, it seemed to foreshadow the typographic free-for-all that was about to be unleashed by computer programs such as Fontographer; and whether one found Ed's work intriguing or ugly and scary had a lot to do with where one fell, generationally, in the acceptance of the new digital tools.

In the lettering samples in this book, then, one can see the evidence of both the completely hand-drawn letters and the manipulated fonts. Fella still uses both techniques interchangeably and tirelessly, without the aid of computers. Very, very little of what he designs is produced for paying clients: in most of Fella's work these days he is his own client. His copious reading of poetry and literary theory is often expressed through the strange and oblique phrases he uses in his announcements. This creates a tension with the forms of the letters conveying the words, which are far removed from the convention of typographic neutrality used to convey even the most sophisticated poetic language.

Fella's collection of Polaroid pictures of lettering works alongside what he does on his drawing-board and in the notebooks. He does not really claim the photographs as a body of artistic work, but it is not purely research, either, at least in the way that most people understand how research is supposed to have a direct relationship to new work produced. Nor is it exactly a picture archive, in that he does not appropriate from it. Maybe the Polaroids are the embodiment of a graphic designer's performance art: deeply committed, regularly performed acts of observation, a harder and rarer practice to maintain in this age of stock and copyright-free imagery that designers so often utilize but don't really see. Looking at the lettering and the Polaroids together, it is difficult to imagine either one of them existing without the other; but it is Fella's faithfulness to his subject, and his imaginative re-interpretation of its possibilities (evident in the great range of variation in the fragments) that has liberated him to be able to produce what he does, back on the drawing-board, with his circle guides and ball-point pens.

When the graphic design history of the final two decades of the twentieth century is written, the big story will be about the technological revolution in the way that graphic design is made. As digital technology has turned control and responsibility for almost every aspect of production, craft and detail back to the designers and their computers, it is wonderfully ironic that some of the most persuasive and poetic work dealing with this new world has been created by Edward Fella, an 'art designer' stubbornly insisting on an exploration of what can be generated purely with the old-school tools of the brain and eye and hand, with acknowledgement of design culture and history, but without obedience to any old (or new) design ideologies,   of course.

Quality Car & Detailing

Business
Ph. 374-4214

BUCKMASTERS MEMBER

STOP!
O CUSTOMER VEHICLES
AST THIS POINT
STOP !
STOP
CAUTION

Sportif
athletic wear

Reebok   NEW BALANCE
AVIA   WIDE SELECTION
adidas   SPECIAL PRICES   NIKE
Saucony   Etonic

DOWNSTAIRS   99 Mt Auburn
HOURS: Mon-Sat
*Thurs until 8 pm
Sun - 12-6

DRY ICE

212 673-4

HAY AND GRAIN
TOP
KINGS LIQUOR
Cigars and Tobacco.
HARDWARE
OLK ST.

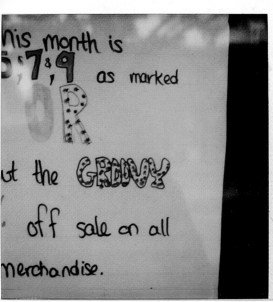

his month is
5, 7, 9 as marked
OR
ut the GROOVY
off sale on all
merchandise.

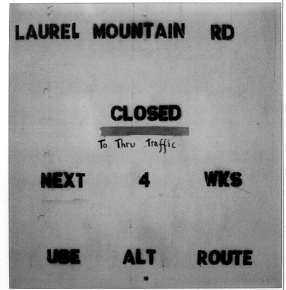

LAUREL MOUNTAIN RD

CLOSED

To Thru Traffic

NEXT   4   WKS

USE   ALT   ROUTE

CORN BEEF
PASTRAMI
BRISKET

BAR PASTA MEAT BALLS
BEEF STEW RIBS

STAGE
AND
VERY ENTRANCE

uB OHM

secured by ADT

RIGHT ON!

218 SE FIFTH

Suite 2

Peace Pot
Pussy
Buy
A
Rubber Perversi
TEMPER
TANTRUM

Doll Sale

GHOST
Ayers

NO EPITAPH
ND NO NAME

PROGRESS

DO NOT ENTER

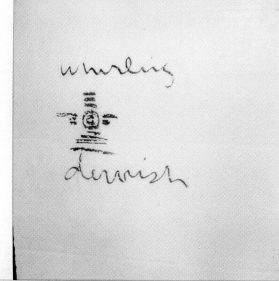
whirling dervish

LORE
TS

UP1ZZA

TOM HOUSE
Y STATE H
PARK

nea

E FOOD ~ SPIRI

Y'S
-CHERY

IL FORNA
RESTAU

THERS WILL BE CIT

ANDYOR
TOWED
M.B.P.D.
543-4566

ORIENTAL
RUGS

769-8555

irst
he hundred

Years

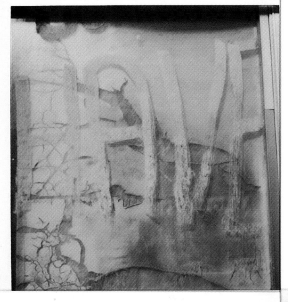
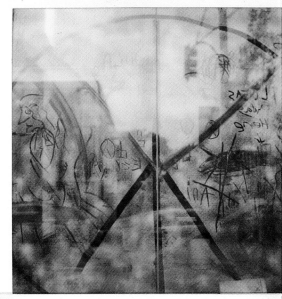

design and typography: Lorraine Wild with Edward Fella
concept and paste-up: Edward Fella

cover design:
with Lorraine Wild and Lucy Bates